SpringerBriefs in Information Systems

Series Editor

Jörg Becker, Münster, Germany

SpringerBriefs present concise summaries of cutting-edge research and practical applications across a wide spectrum of fields. Featuring compact volumes of 50 to 125 pages, the series covers a range of content from professional to academic. Typical topics might include: A timely report of state-of-the art analytical techniques, a bridge between new research results, as published in journal articles, and a contextual literature review, a snapshot of a hot or emerging topic, an in-depth case study or practical example, a presentation of core concepts that students must understand in order to make independent contributions. SpringerBriefs in Information Systems showcase emerging theory, empirical research, and practical application in all subcategories of information systems and related fields, from a global author community. Briefs are characterized by fast, global electronic dissemination, standard publishing contracts, standardized manuscript preparation and formatting guidelines, and expedited production schedules.

Michele Cipriano

Digital Transformation in Non-profit Organizations

A Multi-Layered Perspective

Springer

Michele Cipriano
Department of Economic and
Social Sciences (DiSES)
Catholic University of the
Sacred Heart
Piacenza, Italy

ISSN 2192-4929 ISSN 2192-4937 (electronic)
SpringerBriefs in Information Systems
ISBN 978-3-032-20936-8 ISBN 978-3-032-20937-5 (eBook)
https://doi.org/10.1007/978-3-032-20937-5

This Springer imprint is published by the registered company Springer Nature Switzerland AG
The registered company address is: Gewerbestrasse 11, 6330 Cham, Switzerland

Foreword

Digital transformation (DT) has emerged as one of the defining organizational phenomena of the twenty-first century. Through the pervasive diffusion of digital technologies, it has reshaped industries, institutional arrangements, and patterns of social interaction, altering how value is created, delivered, and sustained. Scholarly research has extensively explored these dynamics within for-profit firms and public sector organizations, where efficiency, competitiveness, and measurable performance outcomes typically dominate analytical frameworks. By contrast, the digital transformation of non-profit organizations (NPOs) has received comparatively limited and fragmented attention, despite the central role these organizations play in addressing complex societal challenges, delivering essential services, and advancing values such as equity, inclusion, and collective well-being.

This book addresses this imbalance by offering a systematic and multi-level examination of digital transformation in non-profit organizations. It is grounded in the recognition that NPOs operate under distinctive organizational, cultural, and ecosystemic conditions that profoundly shape both their opportunities for and constraints on digital change. Mission-driven logics, resource dependencies, governance arrangements, and pluralistic stakeholder environments differentiate NPOs from both for-profit and public sector organizations, rendering the uncritical application of prevailing digital transformation models analytically insufficient and not appropriate. The volume therefore adopts a context-sensitive perspective, conceptualizing digital transformation in NPOs as a socially embedded, strategically negotiated, and institutionally constrained process.

The book builds on a sequence of exploratory and empirical studies that integrate bibliometric analysis, meta-synthesis of prior research, conceptual comparison, and qualitative case-based inquiry. This methodological layering is reflected in the structure of the theoretical contributions developed throughout the chapters, culminating in a multi-layered conceptual framework for understanding digital transformation in non-profit organizations. The framework places foundational organizational preconditions at its core, connects them to strategic logics of digital engagement, and situates observable transformation pathways within a broader set of theoretical dimensions that function as interpretive boundaries. In doing so, the book offers both an analytical lens for scholars and a structured point of reference for practitioners and policymakers.

Across the volume, three interrelated objectives guide the analysis. First, the book consolidates and extends a fragmented body of knowledge on digital transformation in the non-profit domain, contributing conceptual clarity and analytical integration. Second, it differentiates NPO-specific transformation trajectories from dominant for-profit-centric models, foregrounding the role of mission, values, legitimacy, and institutional embeddedness alongside technological capability and strategic intent. Third, it provides empirically grounded insights into how non-profit organizations navigate the enduring tensions between mission fulfilment, resource constraints, and the increasing demands of a digitally mediated society.

Although the analytical orientation of the book is international, the empirical investigations focus primarily on non-profit organizations operating in the United Kingdom. This focus allows for in-depth, contextually grounded analysis of how structural conditions, cultural dynamics, and ecosystem relationships influence digital transformation trajectories. The cases presented throughout the book highlight the iterative interplay between readiness and action, the reciprocal shaping of strategy and organizational capability, and the non-linear, path-dependent character of transformation processes in mission-driven and resource-constrained contexts.

The content of this book contributes to increasing the visibility of non-profit organizations within the broader digital transformation research agenda, positioning them as analytically relevant and theoretically consequential actors of digital change. By developing a coherent conceptual framework and grounding it in systematic empirical inquiry, the volume offers a substantive contribution to an area of research that remains underdeveloped and conceptually dispersed. At the same time, it opens avenues for further empirical, theoretical, and comparative investigation across organizational forms, sectors, and institutional contexts. Beyond its scholarly contribution, the book provides practitioners and policymakers with analytically informed insights that can support reflective decision-making and strengthen the capacity of non-profit organizations to engage with digital transformation in ways that remain aligned with their social missions.

Department of Management and Business Administration
University "G. d'Annunzio",
Pescara, Italy

Stefano Za

Preface

This book is the outcome of a research effort aimed at understanding how non-profit organizations engage with digital transformation (DT) under conditions that differ markedly from those of for-profit firms and public sector institutions. The motivation for this work stems from the observation that digital initiatives in non-profit contexts are often shaped by mission-driven priorities, governance arrangements, and resource constraints that complicate both strategic decision-making and implementation processes. These characteristics raise important questions about how DT initiatives should be conceptualized and examined in organizations whose primary orientation is not economic performance but social value creation.

The book approaches DT in non-profit organizations (NPOs) as a process that unfolds through the interaction of organizational conditions, strategic choices, and contextual influences. Rather than treating technology adoption as a discrete, structured, or linear phenomenon, the analysis is grounded in the assumption that transformation emerges over time, through iterative cycles of experimentation, adjustment, and learning. This perspective reflects the empirical realities observed across different organizational settings, where digital change is rarely uniform and is often negotiated among multiple stakeholders with diverse expectations and constraints.

From a methodological standpoint, the book draws on a combination of complementary approaches. These include structured engagement with existing research, comparative examination of conceptual perspectives, and qualitative empirical analysis. The intention is not to privilege a single method or explanatory lens, but to assemble an analytical foundation that allows for both abstraction and contextual sensitivity. This orientation informs the conceptual architecture discussed throughout the book and shapes the interpretation of the empirical material.

The empirical focus is primarily on NPOs operating in the United Kingdom. This choice enables a detailed examination of how institutional environments, funding arrangements, and ecosystem relationships influence DT processes in practice. The cases discussed illustrate that organizational readiness and strategic intent evolve alongside digital initiatives, reinforcing the view of transformation as a dynamic and path-dependent process rather than a predefined trajectory.

This book is addressed to readers with different backgrounds and interests. Scholars may find the analytical framework useful for interpreting DT phenomena in non-profit contexts and for identifying avenues for further research. Practitioners and policymakers may draw on the empirical illustrations and conceptual distinctions to reflect on their own organizational challenges and strategic choices. Throughout the book, the emphasis is placed on offering points of reference rather than prescriptive solutions, acknowledging the diversity of NPOs and the contexts in which they operate.

In terms of structure, the book is organized to guide the reader progressively from foundational considerations to applied analysis. The opening chapters introduce the conceptual background and clarify the analytical perspective adopted. Subsequent chapters elaborate the core dimensions of the framework and examine how they interact across different organizational settings. The later chapters draw on empirical material to illustrate distinct transformation pathways, before concluding with a discussion of broader implications and directions for future inquiry.

By focusing on the specificities of NPOs, this book aims to support a more nuanced understanding of DT as an organizational and institutional process. It is intended as a resource for readers interested in exploring how digital change is interpreted, enacted, and sustained in contexts where technological innovation intersects with social purpose.

Piacenza, Italy Michele Cipriano

Acknowledgements

This book is the result of a long research journey undertaken as part of my doctoral studies. I wish to express my deepest gratitude to my doctoral supervisor, Professor Stefano Za, whose insight, constructive critique, and constant encouragement have been invaluable throughout this journey. I also extend my thanks to the non-profit organizations and professionals who generously shared their time, perspectives, and experiences, without which the empirical components of this work would not have been possible.

Finally, I am genuinely grateful to my colleagues, friends, and family for their intellectual, practical, and moral support throughout the long process of researching and writing this work. Above all, my profound thanks go to my beloved Elisa, whose unwavering love, patience, and encouragement have been my anchor and inspiration; without you, this journey, and indeed my entire career, would have been unimaginable.

Competing Interests The author has no competing interests to declare that are relevant to the content of this manuscript.

Contents

Chapter 1
Introduction

1.1 Motivations and Research Objectives

In recent decades, the digitization of information has become progressively faster and cheaper, transforming the daily activities of people and organizations through the use of digital technology (Yoo, 2010). The intertwining of "society" and "technology" generates new assets and ecosystems of supply, demand, and exchange, influencing the way economic and social relationships are developed, maintained, and located (OECD, 2019). Among others, digital transformation (DT) phenomena have increasingly affected organizations as well as the whole of society, generating several implications for individuals, institutions, and communities (Carroll et al., 2023).

The academic community has investigated such phenomena extensively, producing multiple definitions. For example, Li et al. (2018) define DT as a transformation "*precipitated by a transformational information technology*" that affects an organization by changing processes, routines, capabilities, markets, and information flows. Zhang et al. (2023) emphasize the "*drastically transformational influence*" of digital technology on firms. Many scholars recognize DT as an IT-driven phenomenon (Legner et al., 2017), involving organizational resources and processes (Baiyere et al., 2020), people and their interactions (Carillo et al., 2017), and sometimes disrupting existing structure and business model (Zimmer et al., 2023). Vial's (2019) widely cited definition conceptualizes DT as a process aimed at improving an entity (such as a process, business unit, or organizational elements) while triggering significant changes in its properties.

Scholarly investigations have addressed DT in specific domains such as financial markets (Currie et al., 2018), healthcare (Ologeanu-Taddei et al., 2023; Pouloudi et al., 2016), and governments (Hofmann et al., 2019; Weerakkody et al., 2016). Some authors argue for the integration of concepts from multiple research areas to understand DT more holistically (Graf-Drasch et al., 2022; Schiliro, 2022).

M. Cipriano, *Digital Transformation in Non-profit Organizations*, SpringerBriefs in Information Systems,
https://doi.org/10.1007/978-3-032-20937-5_1

Organization-centric approaches (Hofmann et al., 2019; Jöhnk et al., 2020; Trenkle, 2019) highlight the need for detailed contextual knowledge (Remane et al., 2017) to identify exogenous and endogenous changes shaping contemporary DT processes (Werle & Laumer, 2022).

Recent socioeconomic and geopolitical challenges (Baiyere et al., 2022), including the COVID-19 pandemic, have accelerated the need for DT, prompting organizations to rebuild postpandemic operations with more agile and resilient settings (Ciccarino & da Silva, 2021; Fletcher & Griffiths, 2020). Global priorities such as resilience, social equity, and inclusion are now considered essential premises for sustainable societal development (Lumpkin & Bacq, 2019; Nogueira et al., 2023). Consequently, practitioners and academics increasingly acknowledge the multiscale and multilevel nature of the stimuli and effects influencing contemporary DT processes (Currie et al., 2022; Gopal et al., 2023).

DT processes hold potential to create both social and economic value (Madon & Schoemaker, 2021), enabling organizations to respond to citizens' needs in the digital era (Ponzoa et al., 2023) and to support recovery and the "good life" (Nogueira et al., 2023). These aims align strongly with the reason d'être of nonprofit organizations (NPOs) (Jeong & Cui, 2020). However, despite the claimed transformative potential of DT for all organizational forms (Carroll et al., 2023), disparities persist in digital maturity and adoption (Ponzoa et al., 2023). For example, while increasing importance is given to NPOs, which play a critical role in contributing to addressing social challenges (Bartosova & Podhorska, 2021), only a limited proportion succeed in implementing functional DT processes (Zaitsev & Mankinen, 2022).

Although DT in the public and for-profit sectors has been extensively studied (Gopal et al., 2023; Warner & Wäger, 2019), the processes through which NPOs navigate DT remain under-researched (Brink et al., 2020; Vogelsang et al., 2021). Little is known about how NPO-specific preconditions and unique value creation logics shape their DT strategies (Brink et al., 2020) or about their pathways for strategic development (Vogelsang et al., 2021).

Research on DT in NPOs is complicated by the heterogeneity of such a sector, distinctive legal and institutional characteristics (Nahrkhalaji et al., 2019), and variable definitions across contexts worldwide (Raghavan et al., 2021; Salamon et al., 2022). NPOs' operations and significance vary widely across geographic and sociopolitical environments (Bartosova & Podhorska, 2021), making the establishment of a unified analytical framework difficult (Carroll, 2020; Carroll et al., 2021).

Besides, technological advances, including cloud-based services and open-source software (Alnamrouti et al., 2022; Tan et al., 2021), have expanded NPOs' capacity for DT compared to a decade ago (Hardiyanto et al., 2023; McNutt et al., 2018). Many NPOs employ technology to develop new or improved services (Gray et al., 2021), strengthen stakeholder relationships (Ihm & Lee, 2021; Zhou & Ye, 2021), and promote their mission through participatory platforms such as social media (Tan et al., 2021). Nevertheless, resource scarcity and skills gaps remain significant barriers (Brink et al., 2020).

Although NPOs may resemble other organizations in certain operational aspects (Vogelsang et al., 2021), their distinctive mission-driven, nondistributive nature

(Bartosova & Podhorska, 2021) differentiates them profoundly from public and for-profit entities (Raghavan et al., 2021; Salamon et al., 2022). Salamon and Sokolowski's (2016) structural/operational definition recognizes NPOs as institutions that are private, self-governing, nonprofit-distributing, and voluntary in participation.

Notwithstanding their unique role and constraints, the implications of DT for NPOs, particularly in relation to global priorities, resilience, and well-being, remain insufficiently explored. There is limited understanding of how DT reshapes service design, production, and delivery in the nonprofit sector (Bogers et al., 2022), even though such processes have evolving and dynamic consequences (Monteiro et al., 2022). Without a close examination of DT in NPOs, there is a risk that stakeholders may fail to realize its full potential for value creation. Thus, room for further investigation refers to enriching our understanding of how DT processes generate new assets and ecosystems for NPOs (Hanelt et al., 2021; Wessel et al., 2021), where their relationships are developed, maintained, and located (OECD, 2019).

1.2 Book Structure

This book aims to enrich and expand the understanding of recent advancements in the discourse on DT initiatives by focusing on the specific context of NPOs. It adopts an organization-centric approach, referring exclusively to NPOs as a distinct ("niche") subtheme of DT research. The work follows a sequence of exploratory and empirical studies, progressing from literature analysis to conceptual development and empirical validation.

Different steps of qualitative and quantitative analysis are first undertaken to provide a systematic understanding of the pertinent scientific literature. This is followed by a multiple-case study investigation designed to reveal implications for the design and development of DT initiatives in NPOs. Accordingly, the book is structured into five main analytical chapters (Chaps. 2–6, as in Fig. 1.1), each addressing a specific step of analysis. A brief description and abstract of each chapter are provided below, with the research question (RQ) explicitly stated.

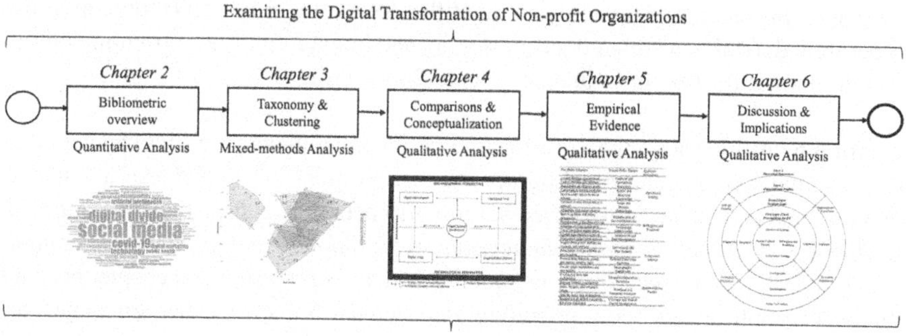

Fig. 1.1 The analytical process through the structure of the book

Chapter 2 Specific attention has recently been paid to the DT process of NPOs, considering that distinct aspects shape DT outcomes in this context. This chapter contributes to the literature by performing a bibliometric and thematic analysis of scholarly publications directly addressing DT in NPOs. This study aims to answer the following *RQ: What are the main research themes, patterns, and trends in the scholarly literature on DT in NPOs?* Thus, the study quantitatively maps the discourse, identifying thematic structures and intellectual clusters in the field. Limitations and opportunities for further research are discussed.

Chapter 3 In a postpandemic society, increasing attention is given to nonprofit-driven DT processes, which must respond to socioeconomic, geopolitical, and technological pressures. Complementing the bibliometric mapping, this chapter undertakes a meta-synthesis of the literature and develops a taxonomy to classify DT initiatives in NPOs. This study aims to answer to the following *RQ: What common characteristics, thematic directions, and patterns emerge from the literature on DT in NPOs?* For this purpose, a cluster analysis is applied to the taxonomy, which led to reasoning on three overarching strategic orientations (i.e., how, who, and what to change), highlighting dominant pathways in DT adoption in NPOs.

Chapter 4 Strategic considerations are widely emphasized in the DT literature on for-profit organizations; however, their relevance and characteristics in the nonprofit context remain unclear. This chapter compares two conceptual frameworks to assess the strategic dimension of DT in NPOs. Then, this study aims to answer the following *RQ: How do the strategic dimensions of DT, widely emphasized in for-profit contexts, differ in their relevance and manifestation in NPOs (given their specific mission-oriented environments)?* As a result, the analysis highlights key divergences between for-profit and nonprofit orientations and proposes an adapted analytical lens tailored to the strategic realities of NPOs.

Chapter 5 To examine DT processes in practice, this chapter presents a cross-sectoral comparison of ten UK-based NPOs. The case study design builds on the conceptual framework from Chap. 4 and investigates how operational conditions shape strategic approaches. Thus, this study aims to answer the following *RQ: How do NPOs operationalize DT processes in practice, and what factors shape their strategic approaches?* The analysis identifies four categories of DT preconditions (operational, readiness-related, ecosystemic, and human-cultural), providing empirical grounding for the subsequent conceptual synthesis.

Chapter 6 Aiming at synthesizing the findings of previous chapters, this chapter introduces a multilayered conceptual framework that positions DT in NPOs as a dynamic, iterative, and context-sensitive process. From this perspective, this study poses the following *RQ: What are the main managerial, organizational, and research implications of DT in NPOs, and what directions should future research take?* The chapter presents the major result of this book, providing a conceptual framework that articulates key tensions in DT processes and integrates theoretical, managerial, and organizational perspectives. Besides, a forward-looking research agenda is ultimately outlined.

References

Alnamrouti, A., Rjoub, H., & Ozgit, H. (2022). Do strategic human resources and artificial intelligence help to make organisations more sustainable? Evidence from Non-Governmental Organisations. *Sustainability, 14*(12), 7327. https://doi.org/10.3390/su14127327

Baiyere, A., Mosconi, E., Wessel, L., & Indulska, M. (2022). Frontiers in digital transformation research. *Information Systems Journal.*

Baiyere, A., Salmela, H., & Tapanainen, T. (2020). Digital transformation and the new logics of business process management. *European Journal of Information Systems, 29*(3), 238–259. https://doi.org/10.1080/0960085X.2020.1718007

Bartosova, V., & Podhorska, I. (2021). The importance of non-profit organization in globalized world: International comparison of American and European continent. *SHS Web of Conferences, 92*, 07008.

Bogers, M. L. A. M., Garud, R., Thomas, L. D. W., Tuertscher, P., & Yoo, Y. (2022). Digital innovation: Transforming research and practice. *Innovation, 24*(1), 4–12. https://doi.org/10.1080/14479338.2021.2005465

Brink, H., Packmohr, S., & Vogelsang, K. (2020). Fields of action to advance the digital transformation of NPOs – Development of a framework. In *Lecture Notes in Business Information Processing* (Vol. 398, pp. 82–97). https://doi.org/10.1007/978-3-030-61140-8_6

Carillo, K., Scornavacca, E., & Za, S. (2017). The role of media dependency in predicting continuance intention to use ubiquitous media systems. *Information and Management, 54*(3), 317–335. https://doi.org/10.1016/j.im.2016.09.002

Carroll, N. (2020). Theorizing on the normalization of digital transformations. In *Twenty-Eighth European Conference on Information Systems (ECIS) – A Virtual AIS Conference.*

Carroll, N., Hassan, N. R., Junglas, I., Hess, T., & Morgan, L. (2021). Managing and sustaining digital transformations. *European Journal of Information Systems.*

Carroll, N., Hassan, N. R., Junglas, I., Hess, T., & Morgan, L. (2023). Transform or be transformed: The importance of research on managing and sustaining digital transformations. *European Journal of Information Systems, 32*(3), 347–353. https://doi.org/10.1080/0960085X.2023.2187033

Ciccarino, I., & da Silva, C. D. S. (2021). Digital transformation: Is it part of a strategic process or a new strategic practice? In *Cases on digital strategies and management issues in modern organizations* (pp. 1–22). IGI Global. https://doi.org/10.4018/978-1-7998-1630-0.ch001

Currie, W., Gozman, D. P., & Seddon, J. J. M. (2018). Dialectic tensions in the financial markets: A longitudinal study of pre- and post-crisis regulatory technology. *Journal of Information Technology, 33*(4), 304–325. https://doi.org/10.1057/s41265-017-0047-5

Currie, W. L., Hsu, C., van Vliet, B., & Weerakkody, V. (2022). Digital transformation as geopolitical, organizational and technological nexus. *Journal of Information Technology.*

Fletcher, G., & Griffiths, M. (2020). Digital transformation during a lockdown. *International Journal of Information Management, 55*, 102185. https://doi.org/10.1016/j.ijinfomgt.2020.102185

Gopal, R. D., Hidaji, H., Kutlu, S. N., Patterson, R. A., & Yaraghi, N. (2023). Law, economics, and privacy: Implications of government policies on website and third-party information sharing. *Information Systems Research, March*, 1–23. https://doi.org/10.1287/isre.2022.1178

Graf-Drasch, V., Krombacher, A., Lindenthal, A., Oberländer, A. M., & Schäfer, R. (2022). Digitally social: Review, synthesis, and future directions for digital social innovation. In *30h European Conference on Information Systems (ECIS)*. Timişoara.

Gray, F. E., Murray, N., & Hopkins, K. (2021). Affordances of e-newsletters for NPO general-public stakeholders. *VOLUNTAS: International Journal of Voluntary and Nonprofit Organizations, 32*(5), 1165–1181. https://doi.org/10.1007/s11266-021-00374-2

Hanelt, A., Bohnsack, R., Marz, D., & Antunes Marante, C. (2021). A systematic review of the literature on digital transformation: Insights and implications for strategy and organizational change. *Journal of Management Studies, 58*(5), 1159–1197. https://doi.org/10.1111/joms.12639

Hardiyanto, N., Ahmar, N., & Etty Merawati, E. (2023). Internet financial report and determinants of the quality of financial statements of non-profit organizations. *Devotion Journal of Community Service, 4*(1), 186–201. https://doi.org/10.36418/dev.v4i1.369

Hofmann, S., Sæbø, Ø., Braccini, A. M., & Za, S. (2019). The public sector's roles in the sharing economy and the implications for public values. *Government Information Quarterly, 36*(4), 101399. https://doi.org/10.1016/j.giq.2019.101399

Ihm, J., & Lee, S. (2021). How perceived costs and benefits of initial social media participation affect subsequent community-based participation. *VOLUNTAS: International Journal of Voluntary and Nonprofit Organizations, 32*(6), 1320–1331. https://doi.org/10.1007/s11266-020-00200-1

Jeong, J., & Cui, T. S. (2020). The density of nonprofit organizations: Beyond community diversity and resource availability. *VOLUNTAS: International Journal of Voluntary and Nonprofit Organizations, 31*(1), 213–226. https://doi.org/10.1007/s11266-019-00175-8

Jöhnk, J., Ollig, P., Oesterle, S., & Riedel, L. N. (2020). The Complexity of Digital Transformation-Conceptualizing Multiple Concurrent Initiatives. In *Wirtschaftsinformatik (Zentrale Tracks)* (pp. 1051–1066).

Legner, C., Eymann, T., Hess, T., Matt, C., Bo, T., Urbach, N., et al. (2017). Digitalisation: Opportunity and challenge for the business and information systems engineering community. *Business and Information Systems Engineering, 59*(4), 301–308. https://doi.org/10.1007/s12599-017-0484-2

Li, L., Su, F., Zhang, W., & Mao, J.-Y. (2018). Digital transformation by SME entrepreneurs: A capability perspective. *Information Systems Journal, 28*(6), 1129–1157. https://doi.org/10.1111/isj.12153

Lumpkin, G. T., & Bacq, S. (2019). Civic wealth creation: A new view of stakeholder engagement and societal impact. *Academy of Management Perspectives, 33*(4), 383–404. https://doi.org/10.5465/amp.2017.0060

Madon, S., & Schoemaker, E. (2021). Digital identity as a platform for improving refugee management. *Information Systems Journal, 31*(6), 929–953. https://doi.org/10.1111/isj.12353

McNutt, J., Guo, C., Goldkind, L., & An, S. (2018). Technology in nonprofit organizations and voluntary action. *Voluntaristics Review, 3*(1), 1–63. https://doi.org/10.1163/24054933-12340020

Monteiro, E., Constantinides, P., Scott, S., Shaikh, M., & Burton-Jones, A. (2022). Qualitative research methods in information systems: A call for phenomenon-focused problematization. *MIS Quarterly, 46*(4), i–xviii.

Nahrkhalaji, S. S., Shafiee, S., Shafiee, M., & Hvam, L. (2019). Challenges of digital transformation: The case of the non-profit sector. In *Proceedings of 2018 IEEE International Conference on Industrial Engineering and Engineering Management (IEEM)*.

Nogueira, C., Marques, J. F., & Pinto, H. (2023). Civil economy as a path towards sustainability: An empirical investigation. *Journal of Cleaner Production, 383*(November 2022), 135486.

OECD. (2019). Vectors of digital transformation. *OECD Digital Economy Papers, 273*, 1–38. https://doi.org/10.1787/20716826

Ologeanu-Taddei, R., Guthrie, C., & Jensen, T. B. (2023). Digital transformation of professional healthcare practices: Fitness seeking across a rugged value landscape. *European Journal of Information Systems, 32*(3), 354–371. https://doi.org/10.1080/0960085X.2023.2165978

Ponzoa, J. M., Gómez, A., & Mas, J. M. (2023). EU27 and USA institutions in the digital ecosystem: Proposal for a digital presence measurement index. *Journal of Business Research, 154*(2023), 113354. https://doi.org/10.1016/j.jbusres.2022.113354

Pouloudi, N., Currie, W., & Whitley, E. (2016). Entangled stakeholder roles and perceptions in health information systems: A longitudinal study of the U.K. NHS N3 network. *Journal of the Association for Information Systems, 17*(2), 107–161. https://doi.org/10.17705/1jais.00421

Raghavan, A., Demircioglu, M. A., & Orazgaliyev, S. (2021). COVID-19 and the new normal of organizations and employees: An overview. *Sustainability, 13*(21), 11942. https://doi.org/10.3390/su132111942

Remane, G., Hanelt, A., Wiesboeck, F., & Kolbe, L. (2017). Digital maturity in traditional industries: An exploratory analysis. In *25th European Conference on Information Systems (ECIS)*. Guimarães.

Salamon, L. M., Haddock, M. A., & Toepler, S. (2022). Conceptualizing, measuring, and theorizing the third sector: Embedding statistical and methodological developments awaiting broader scholarly take-up. *VOLUNTAS: International Journal of Voluntary and Nonprofit Organizations*. https://doi.org/10.1007/s11266-022-00468-5

Salamon, L. M., & Sokolowski, S. W. (2016). Beyond nonprofits: Re-conceptualizing the Third Sector. *VOLUNTAS: International Journal of Voluntary and Nonprofit Organizations, 27*(4), 1515–1545. https://doi.org/10.1007/s11266-016-9726-z

Schiliro, D. (2022). Digital economy and digital transformation. In *Digital Technologies for Entrepreneurship in Industry 4.0* (pp. 26–42). IGI Global. https://doi.org/10.4018/978-1-6684-4265-4.ch002

Tan, X., Lu, Y., & Tan, Y. (2021). The impact of subscription reciprocity on charitable content creation and sharing: Evidence from Twitter on Giving Tuesday. *MIS Quarterly, 45*(2), 535–562.

Trenkle, J. (2019). Survival in the digital age – A framework for formulating a Digital Transformation Strategy in SME, In *Proceedings of The 19th International Conference on Electronic Business* (pp. 428–442). ICEB, Newcastle upon Tyne, UK, December 8–12. ICEB proceedings.

Vial, G. (2019). Understanding digital transformation: A review and a research agenda. *Journal of Strategic Information Systems, 28*(2), 118–144. https://doi.org/10.1016/j.jsis.2019.01.003

Vogelsang, K., Packmohr, S., & Brink, H. (2021). Challenges of the digital transformation – Comparing nonprofit and industry organizations. In *Lecture Notes in Information Systems and Organisation* (Vol. 46, pp. 297–312). https://doi.org/10.1007/978-3-030-86790-4_21

Warner, K. S. R., & Wäger, M. (2019). Building dynamic capabilities for digital transformation: An ongoing process of strategic renewal. *Long Range Planning, 52*(3), 326–349. https://doi.org/10.1016/j.lrp.2018.12.001

Weerakkody, V., Omar, A., El-Haddadeh, R., & Al-Busaidy, M. (2016). Digitally-enabled service transformation in the public sector: The lure of institutional pressure and strategic response towards change. *Government Information Quarterly, 33*(4), 658–668. https://doi.org/10.1016/j.giq.2016.06.006

Werle, M., & Laumer, S. (2022). Competitor identification: A review of use cases, data sources, and algorithms. *International Journal of Information Management, 65*, 102507. https://doi.org/10.1016/j.ijinfomgt.2022.102507

Wessel, L., Baiyere, A., Ologeanu-Taddei, R., Cha, J., & Blegind Jensen, T. (2021). Unpacking the difference between digital transformation and IT-enabled organizational transformation. *Journal of the Association for Information Systems, 22*(1), 102–129. https://doi.org/10.17705/1jais.00655

Yoo, Y. (2010). Computing in everyday life: A call for research on experiential computing. *MIS Quarterly, 34*(2), 213. https://doi.org/10.2307/20721425

Zaitsev, A., & Mankinen, S. (2022). Designing financial education applications for development: Applying action design research in Cambodian countryside. *European Journal of Information Systems, 31*(1), 91–111.

Zhang, Z., Jin, J., Li, S., & Zhang, Y. (2023). Digital transformation of incumbent firms from the perspective of portfolios of innovation. *Technology in Society, 72*, 102149. https://doi.org/10.1016/j.techsoc.2022.102149

Zhou, H., & Ye, S. (2021). Fundraising in the digital era: Legitimacy, social network, and political ties matter in China. *VOLUNTAS: International Journal of Voluntary and Nonprofit Organizations, 32*(2), 498–511. https://doi.org/10.1007/s11266-019-00112-9

Zimmer, M. P., Baiyere, A., & Salmela, H. (2023). Digital workplace transformation: Subtraction logic as deinstitutionalising the taken-for-granted. *The Journal of Strategic Information Systems, 32*(1), 101757.

References

Chapter 2
An Overview of the Scientific Debate

2.1 The Phenomenon and the Context

Over the last few years, the challenges triggered by uncertainty and unexpected events (Aria et al., 2022; Weick & Sutcliffe, 2015), such as the COVID-19 pandemic (Hai et al., 2021; Nagel, 2020), have significantly affected the production of scientific research (Ali, 2022). Among other aspects, in the academic literature, several scholars focus on the need to understand (Hausberg et al., 2019), conceptualize (Jöhnk et al., 2020), and manage (Benbunan-Fich et al., 2020) the changes affecting the organizational ecosystems (vom Brocke & Mendling, 2018). In particular, although the digital transformation (DT) debate is a recurring topic among different fields of study, by exploring organizational antifragility (Munoz et al., 2021, 2022) and envisioning "a new normal" toward resilience, well-being, and Sustainable Development Goals (SDGs) (Ameli et al., 2022; d'Orville, 2020; Obradović et al., 2021; Rapanta et al., 2021), DT initiatives appear to be a global priority nowadays (Carroll, 2020; Pee et al., 2021). The significance of DT initiatives could be seen in facilitating innovation, providing organizational flexibility (Nicholson et al., 2021), and their potential to generate social and economic value (Madon & Schoemaker, 2021; Uzcanga & Oiarzabal, 2019). For instance, some organizations develop DT initiatives to enable organizational changes (Hanelt et al., 2021; Wessel et al., 2021), while others seek to improve their business opportunities (Nwankpa & Roumani, 2016; Schallmo et al., 2017).

The DT phenomenon still represents a thought-provoking topic for academics and practitioners (Gopal et al., 2023), who question its novelty (Baiyere et al., 2023) while examining multiple and interconnected variables affecting its comprehension (Werle & Laumer, 2022). In the last decade, different understandings of DT have been conceptualized by scholars (Markus & Rowe, 2021; Monteiro et al., 2022), adopting a technology-centric approach (Teubner, 2013), a business-centric perspective (Bharadwaj et al., 2013), or a holistic one (Matt et al., 2015). Definitions of

M. Cipriano, *Digital Transformation in Non-profit Organizations*, SpringerBriefs in Information Systems,
https://doi.org/10.1007/978-3-032-20937-5_2

DT take on different rationales (Schallmo et al., 2017; Schiliro, 2022), ranging from an IT-driven phenomenon (Legner et al., 2017; Wiesböck & Hess, 2020) involving multiple entities to the conceptualization of Vial (2019), presenting DT as a process that could improve, transform, or change an entity's property (Vial, 2019). Building on these assumptions, a large body of academic research examines the DT process with regard to different sectors and fields of study (Carroll et al., 2023; Hanelt et al., 2021; Shirish et al., 2023; Verhoef et al., 2021; Wessel et al., 2021). However, some top journal editorials (Markus & Rowe, 2021), special issues (Nicholson et al., 2021; vom Brocke et al., 2020), especially from the information systems (IS) community, invite researchers to expand their insight into the DT process. Specifically, practitioners and academics are increasingly acknowledging a nexus of multiscale and multilevel stimuli and the effects influencing or generating contemporary DT processes (Currie et al., 2022; Gopal et al., 2023). In addition, there is growing recognition of organizations' unequal development and digital presence (Ponzoa et al., 2023), where room for further investigations concerns how to manage and sustain DT processes (Chanias et al., 2019).

Some scholars claim that there are difficulties in conceptualizing DT-enabled change management and implementation (Hanelt et al., 2021; Wessel et al., 2021), also arguing that the DT process seems not to have been well theorized yet (Markus & Rowe, 2021). For example, Trischler and Li-Ying (2022) argue that the lack of specific aspects linked to DT outcomes in a given context makes it difficult to identify DT as applied to such a context. Remané et al. (2017) challenge the idea that DT processes can be evaluated and measured through the same DT path for all firms, stating that the impact of DT processes relies on a firm's digital maturity level and readiness to master the related changes. Furthermore, there is a growing interest in how organizations can access resource management for their DT in dynamic and transient arrangements (Li et al., 2022) since one difficulty concerns the resource fluidity for DT processes (Nadkarni & Prügl, 2021). Other difficulties involve some IS contexts that may not be well understood (Carroll, 2020; Rowe, 2018), perhaps because they do not have a well-defined organizational ecosystem (Carroll, 2020; Cipriano & Za, 2022a, 2022b).

From this perspective, some researchers have discussed the roles of information and communication technologies (ICTs) in a wide range of major societal challenges, providing recommendations for the design of DT processes (Majchrzak et al., 2016). Further scholars have extensively analyzed DT processes and societal challenges with regard to public and for-profit organizations (Gopal et al., 2023; Warner & Wäger, 2019). However, the literature reveals that nonprofit organizations (NPOs) represent a unique context (Cipriano & Za, 2021; Vogelsang et al., 2021) that deserves further investigation concerning the DT discourse and related organizational changes (Brink et al., 2020; Cipriano & Za, 2022a). Some scholars argue that little attention is paid to the DT process with respect to the commitment of NPOs, their organizational operability, and the way they create value (Cipriano & Za, 2022b). NPOs rely predominantly on voluntary participation, work, and membership (Nahrkhalaji et al., 2019). NPOs' operability primarily depends on donations and fundraising, and their activities disregard any consideration or distribution of profit (Cipriano & Za, 2021). NPOs are organizations that, as per their nature, uniquely commit to building civil society and strengthening common well-being, social capital, and economic development (Nahrkhalaji et al., 2019). Although NPOs may operate like any other industry, they are likely to have unique objectives, organizational features, and operability assets (Cipriano & Za, 2022b; Nahrkhalaji et al., 2019). As a consequence, since NPOs are characterized by a "nondistributional constraint" (Taylor, 2010), they differ significantly from other organizational forms, both in the way they achieve their objectives and in their unique raison d'être (Bekkers & Wiepking, 2011; Hansmann, 1981). For these reasons, NPOs may represent an IS context that is still poorly understood, as well as an opportunity to enrich and improve further conceptualization of DT.

In this book, it is questioned whether the existing research is relevant for analyzing and advancing DT initiatives concerning NPOs. Specifically, it attempts to extend the understanding of DT with regard to specific lines of inquiry, exploring a nexus of changes considering the DT diversity (Baiyere et al., 2022; Currie et al., 2022; Tekic & Koroteev, 2019) in the footsteps of Vial's (2019) definition of DT. It seeks to change the frame of analysis from a general for-profit perspective (Hess et al., 2016) to a nonprofit one (Salamon & Sokolowski, 2016), especially considering that their insights from previous research correspond to specific markets and cases analyzed (Chanias et al., 2019; Jöhnk et al., 2020; Wiesböck & Hess, 2020). Hence, this work attempts to challenge and broaden the problematization of the debate on DT related to civic and societal challenges (Majchrzak et al., 2016; Selander & Jarvenpaa, 2016). For example, it seeks to provide an extensive overview of the debate (strictly discussing DT in NPOs), not limited to empirical evidence based on large-scale companies (Selander & Jarvenpaa, 2016). It is not restricted to the level of investigation, for example, considering the involvement of several actors and millions of members and supporters (Selander & Jarvenpaa, 2016). Furthermore, it does not adopt governmental perspectives (Hofmann et al., 2019) or focus on specific initiatives/phenomena such as (1) social media's influence on political activism; (2) Internet access in various countries; (3) refugee families that make use of personal computers and online access; (4) delivering government benefits to citizens in a remote area; (5) comparison of biometric identity verification programs; and (6) focus on specific geographical areas (i.e., Western business contexts) (Majchrzak et al., 2016).

To this end, this first section of the book proposes a literature review based on bibliometric data analysis (Cipriano & Za, 2025) to advance the understanding of themes concerning the evolution of DT research in NPOs (Di Vaio et al., 2023; Kataeva et al., 2023). By adopting this approach, this study seeks to provide a more comprehensive overview of the debate compared with previous qualitative research (Brink et al., 2020; Cipriano & Za, 2022b; Vogelsang et al., 2021). Specifically, this study aims to answer the following research question: What is the trend, and what are the main themes characterizing the DT debate regarding NPOs? To this end, a performance analysis is developed to describe the scientific contributions discussing DT in NPOs, considering different sources and quality of publications, with a particular focus on the IS field (Kataeva et al., 2023). To perform the analysis, the

Bibliometrix package (Aria & Cuccurullo, 2022) in the R environment is used. Following this, a science mapping network analysis, focusing on authors' keyword co-occurrences, aims to investigate the conceptual structure, evolution, and relations between themes.

This chapter is structured as follows. The next subsection summarizes the theoretical development of previous studies to support comprehension of the research design, data analysis, and result interpretation. The methodology subsection and the literature search protocol follow this. The performance and science mapping analysis are provided and discussed in the results subsection. Conclusions concerning such an overview of the scientific discourse close the chapter.

2.2 Theoretical Background

By exploring the literature, it appears that several scholars adopt a bibliometric approach to systematically study scientific publications in relation to a given domain (Bracarense et al., 2022; Cobo et al., 2018; Lamboglia et al., 2021; Scornavacca et al., 2020; Za & Spagnoletti, 2013). Among other statistical techniques, this approach is purposely helpful in exploring the history, the development, and the general state of the art of a specific research field, as well as of topics over a long period (Aria et al., 2020; Cobo et al., 2011; Za, Ghiringhelli, & Virili, 2020a). This technique is based on the analysis of bibliographic material, which is usually collected from online databases (Cobo et al., 2011; Donthu et al., 2020). It consists of different analyses that rely on more basic descriptive analysis of bibliometric data (performance analysis) (Aria et al., 2020; White & McCain, 1998), and more accurate ones for investigating a scientific field and examining an area in relation to its knowledge structure and evolution (science mapping) (Börner et al., 2005; Small, 1999).

Examining existing literature on DT, it appears that there has been a proliferation of bibliometric studies in recent years, with multidisciplinary topics (Chinotaikul & Vinayavekhin, 2020). For example, Chawla and Goyal (2022) analyze 234 journal articles published in the last 20 years. Their research outlines the emerging trends in DT by investigating the citation, co-citation, and keyword analysis (Chawla & Goyal, 2022). de Bem Machado et al. (2022) provide a structured literature review of 761 articles discussing knowledge management, DT, and Industry 4.0 to recognize the interactions and interdependencies of such research streams. These authors adopt a hybrid methodology by using the Bibliometrix R package to increase the study's rigor and decrease its bias (de Bem Machado et al., 2022). In comparison, to develop a systematic literature review, Kraus et al. (2021) adopt the VOS viewer software to analyze the authors' keywords co-occurrences. Specifically, they present a qualitative classification of the DT discussion by recognizing three clusters that represent technological, business, and societal impacts (Kraus et al., 2021). Also, it seems their research could provide helpful insights to the government and private sectors in guiding the management of disruptive changes (Kraus et al.,

2021). Adekunle et al. (2021) focus instead on the DT discussion concerning the construction industry. By classifying the discourse based on the co-occurrence of keywords (authors and journals indexed), their analysis shows an increasing interest in DT initiatives in such an industry over the last 10 years (Adekunle et al., 2021). Since it appears that some existing barriers limit the discussion in some countries, the authors also develop a supporting model and define some areas that require further research (Adekunle et al., 2021).

Furthermore, Pizzi et al. (2021) perform a bibliometric analysis to investigate the impacts caused by DT on managerial auditing. These authors adopt a mixed approach based on bibliometric analysis and literature review to develop more focused research (Pizzi et al., 2021). They perform a citation, keywords, and density analysis (Pizzi et al., 2021), creating a research agenda in addition to outlining four independent research areas of interest: (i) continuous auditing, (ii) fraud detection, (iii) data analytics, and (iv) technological innovation. In comparison, Chinotaikul and Vinayavekhin (2020) explore DT as a field in business and management research. They focused mainly on the co-word network analyses for identifying the influential articles and the intellectual structure of the debate (Chinotaikul & Vinayavekhin, 2020). These authors claim that this is an emerging research field, whose growth has been of particular interest over the last 4 years, especially concerning the Internet of Things (IoT) and digital twin themes (Chinotaikul & Vinayavekhin, 2020).

However, only a few studies explore the DT debate, focusing strictly on NPOs (Brink et al., 2020; Cipriano & Za, 2021, 2022a, 2022b; Nahrkhalaji et al., 2019; Vogelsang et al., 2021), most of which adopt a qualitative approach. It mainly appears that NPOs are significantly active in leveraging digital-based communication to facilitate interactions with their stakeholders; in addition to being particularly involved in providing public service delivery to society. Based on these previous outcomes, the DT phenomenon is here considered as a process, focusing on its potential implications for organizational change (Vial, 2019). Yet, considering that the DT phenomenon differs from past IT-related organizational change (Wessel et al., 2021), it is challenging to analyze DT-enabled change management and change implementation since DT is triggered and shaped by the widespread diffusion of digital technologies (Hanelt et al., 2021). Therefore, regarding the identification of the organizational context, this research adopts the Salamon and Sokolowski conceptualization of NPOs (Salamon & Sokolowski, 2016). Then, NPOs are identified as: (1) *Institutions* (or organizations that could be either formally or legally formed or not), (2) *Private* (institutionally separated and not controlled by government), (3) *Self-governed* (able to control its activities without the operational control by any other entity, private, or governmental), (4) *Nonprofit-distributing* (a legal prohibition is placed on any organization's constituents or other stakeholders from receiving any quota of the surplus generated by the organization's activities), and (5) *Without compulsion* (any participation with the organization has to be voluntary as a matter of free choice). It follows the description of the method.

2.3 Research Method

This study adopts a bibliometric approach to explore the most active research area and the foundations of the DT discourse in NPOs (Castriotta et al., 2019; Cipriano & Za, 2025). In examining the structure and characteristics of topics through the study of scientific publications (Ferreira et al., 2014; Zupic & Čater, 2015), the bibliometric methods are applied in two main usages, performance analysis and science mapping (Cobo et al., 2011). The goal of the study is to explore the conceptual evolution of DT in NPOs and uncover links between concepts through term co-occurrences. For this purpose, the first analysis focuses on describing the distribution of publications among journals, book chapters, and conference proceedings. In doing so, the attempt is to outline the extent of research proliferation in the major IS sources. Among other approaches and available data, subsequent analysis is executed exclusively employing the keywords defined by the authors (i.e., excluding keywords generated from the platform or "indexed keywords"), considering that they are supposed to be the closest representation of a contribution, following the authors' standpoint. A thematic map based on co-word network analysis and clustering of authors' keywords is then proposed (Caputo et al., 2019; Huang et al., 2021; Marzi et al., 2020). That is, keyword networks strongly linked to each other are located (Callon et al., 1991), presenting the resulting diagram. Then, the resulting themes are visualized through a thematic network, identifying clusters representing a research stream, or a subject of significant interest among researchers (Chinotaikul & Vinayavekhin, 2020; Cobo et al., 2018; Lamboglia et al., 2021). Notably, this process is characterized by two measures: centrality and density (Callon et al., 1991; Cobo et al., 2011). As a way of explanation, the clusters of authors' keywords are arranged on a map based on their centrality value (x-axis), density value (y-axis), and occurrence (bubble size) of each cluster (ibid). The first measure, "centrality," represents the importance of a cluster in the development of the whole research domain and the degree of interaction of a network with other networks. The second measure, "density," identifies the internal strength of a network in terms of internal connections between the keywords of a cluster (theme development). The third measure is self-explanatory as it represents the count of keyword occurrences. By using these measures, one could define a set of research themes mapped into a (two-dimensional) strategic diagram as a synthetic representation of a network (Callon et al., 1991). According to Cobo et al. (2011), to analyze the thematic map, one could assign a strategic meaning to each quadrant of the diagram. In doing so, themes could be classified into four groups: (1) *motor themes* (well established and theoretically relevant for the research field), (2) *highly developed and isolated themes* (theoretically relevant but with marginal importance for the research field), (3) *emerging or declining themes* (marginal and weakly established due to an emerging or instead declining theoretical relevance), and (4) *basic transversal themes* (relevant for the research field but poorly developed) (Cobo et al., 2011). Figure 2.1 depicts the research protocol of this study, adapted from Cipriano and Za (2025).

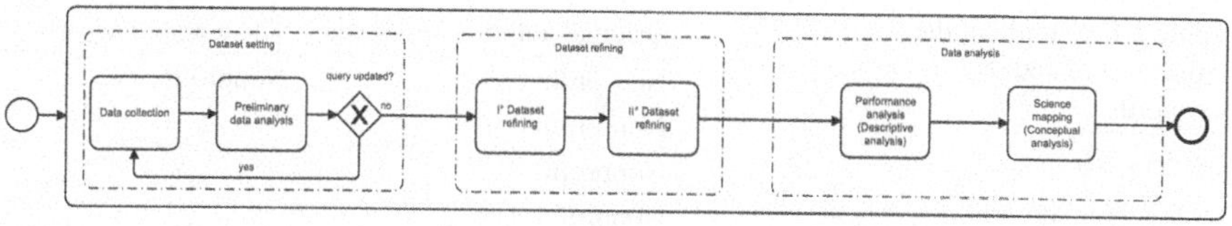

Fig. 2.1 Research protocol (Adapted from Cipriano & Za, 2025)

The research protocol in Fig. 2.1 is based on three main steps: dataset setting, dataset refining, and data analysis. The first step consists of data collection, including identifying a relevant source for the literature search, developing a comprehensive research query, and refining the query keywords manually. The Scopus database was used for collecting the corpus since it is an indexing platform highly deployed by academics and practitioners of social studies (Rahal & Zainuba, 2019). The research query was reiterated several times, using different keywords, to include all the publications that do not focus on DT in any sector but are strongly related to NPOs. Also, keywords such as "ICT" or "IT" were not included as this research considers DT an exclusive phenomenon (Hanelt et al., 2021; Wessel et al., 2021). Ultimately, the final search terms (i.e., *digital transformation* and *nonprofit organization*) were searched in the authors' keywords, title, and abstract (papers') fields, after revising them by using wildcards to include plurals and grammatical and spelling variations. Also, a limitation was set on the language for retrieving papers written only in English.

By running the final query, an initial dataset of 698 contributions was collected, concerning a period automatically established from the search (last updated on May 30, 2022). In the second step, two main refinements of the dataset were performed. The criteria for including, or not, a contribution were first established. For example, journal articles, conference papers, books, book chapters, editorials, and reviews were included. In contrast, conference reviews, notes, short surveys, data papers, errata, and undefined (after analyzing these contributions) were excluded. Moreover, additional excluded contributions were those that lacked the author/s' name. As a result, a refined corpus of 633 papers was obtained.

In the second round of refinement, the number of citations for each document was updated, and some labels of cited sources were homogenized. False positives (e.g., papers including the two keywords but not jointly discussing the two topics) were excluded, and some authors' keywords were cleaned and updated since it emerged that different keywords representing the same topic overlapped among the papers (i.e., synonyms and periphrases). In particular, aimed to keep the authors' closest perspective, the homogenization process sought to homogenize objectively and theoretically similar keywords such as acronyms, singular or plural spelling variations, abbreviations, and etymologically equivalent ones. In doing so, 1882 keywords (different occurrences) were refined to a homogenized set composed of 1808 keywords (see Table 2.1). Moreover, noticing that 170 contributions were missing the author's keywords but were apt for the analysis, a set of representative keywords for each contribution was added to such papers (using only homogenized

Table 2.1 Sample of the refined set of authors' keywords

Original author's keywords	The adopted keyword
Non-profit	Nonprofit
Non-profits	
Nonprofit	
Nonprofits	
Non-for-profit	

keywords). Ultimately, the final corpus used in the following step consisted of 586 contributions.

Finally, in the third step, the software RStudio with the Bibliometrix package (Aria & Cuccurullo, 2017, 2022) was employed to perform the bibliometric analysis, investigating the publication and citation trends (Baier-Fuentes et al., 2019; Za & Braccini, 2017), with an emphasis on the analysis of sources belonging to the IS field of study. Afterward, a co-word analysis focusing on the authors' most frequently used keywords, their co-occurrences, and relations was performed, and followed by a thematic map (Aria et al., 2022; Cobo et al., 2011; Kraus et al., 2022) to analyze the behavior of such a scientific community and the links occurring between the objects of analysis (Ricciardi & Za, 2015; Scornavacca et al., 2020; Za, Ghiringhelli, & Virili, 2020a).

2.4 Results and Discussion

This subsection consists of two parts encompassing the two objectives of the study. The first provides the performance analysis, describing the trend of publications and citations by focusing on the most relevant sources, countries, authors, and cited papers. The second carries on the science mapping analysis, investigating the most influential topics in our dataset based on the most recurring keywords used by authors. It first focuses on the trend of the 41 most used keywords, and then presents the thematic map based on the authors' keywords co-occurrences.

Performance Analysis

This analysis was performed at the beginning of June 2022, focusing on the final dataset of 586 contributions distributed over 462 sources. Figure 2.2 depicts the annual scientific publication trend since 1983, described subsequently.

Figure 2.2 illustrates a rising interest in the discussion on DT focused on NPOs over the past two decades, with slight dips observed in 2015 and 2019. In comparison to previous research (Chawla & Goyal, 2022; Chinotaikul & Vinayavekhin,

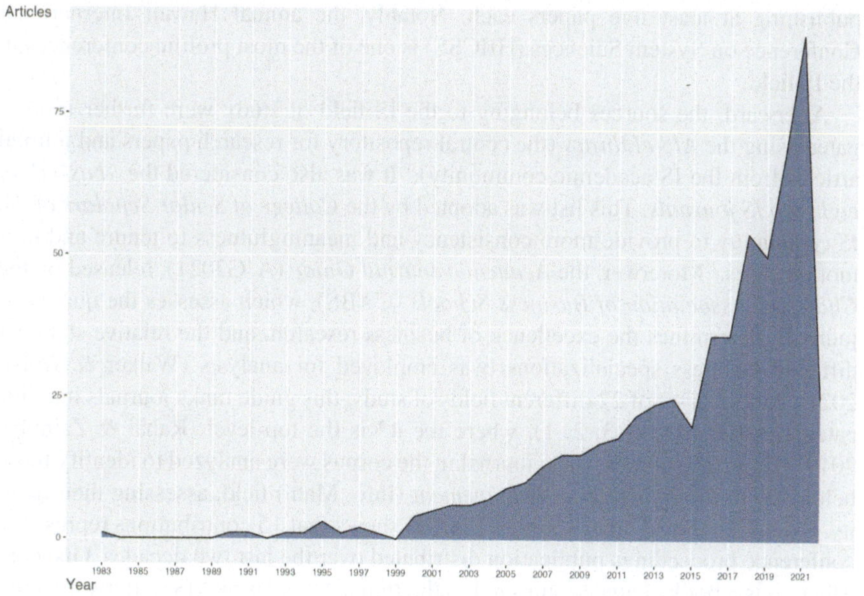

Fig. 2.2 Annual scientific production of the DT research in NPOs from 1983

Table 2.2 Top 9 most relevant sources

Source	Articles
ACM International Conference Proceedings Series	8
Voluntas: International Journal of Voluntary and Nonprofit Organizations	7
Digital Journalism	6
Journalism	6
Telematics And Informatics	6
Ceur Workshop Proceedings	5
Journalism Practice	5
Nonprofit and Voluntary Sector Quarterly	5
Proceedings of the Annual Hawaii International Conference on System Sciences (HICSS)	5

2020) focusing on NPOs, the trend of publications appears to have a marked exponential growth over time, with a notable increase in the number of publications in recent years (especially between 2018 and 2021, representing approximately 50% of the total number of publications). For 2022, the number of publications will likely increase as the year progresses.

By analyzing the most relevant source, it appears that the corpus is distributed over various specializations, developing a multidisciplinary discussion. It emerges that among 462 different sources, only 67 published more than one paper. Specifically, 41 out of 67 sources published two papers, 12 published three, and 5 published four. In comparison, Table 2.2 shows the remaining top 9 sources publishing at least five papers each. Notably, the annual Hawaii International Conference on System Sciences (HIICSS) is one of the most prolific conferences in the IS field.

Afterward, the sources belonging to the IS field of study were further investigated using the *AIS eLibrary* (the central repository for research papers and journal articles from the IS academic community).[1] It was also considered the *"basket" of eight top IS journals*. This list was adopted by the *College of Senior Scholars of the IS community* to provide more consistency and meaningfulness to tenure and promotion cases.[2] Moreover, the *Academic Journal Guide* (AJG2021), released by the *Chartered Association of Business Schools* (CABS), which assesses the quality of journals, determines the excellence of business research, and the relative status of different business specializations, was employed for analysis (Walker & Wood, 2021). Among a set of 22 different fields of study, this guide ranks journals into five categories (i.e., 4*, 4, 3, 2, 1), where the 4* is the top-level (Rahal & Zainuba, 2019). Then, the sources of the journal in the corpus were analyzed to identify those belonging to the *Information Management* (Info. Man.) field, assessing their quality. Excluding the 30 other sources, Fig. 2.3 shows that 15 contributions represent a conference proceedings publication distributed over the last two decades. One contribution is a book chapter connected to the Italian Chapter of AIS. Afterward, considering the journal articles, the *Information Systems Research* journal is assigned one publication. This journal is classified as a 4* journal in the AJG2021,

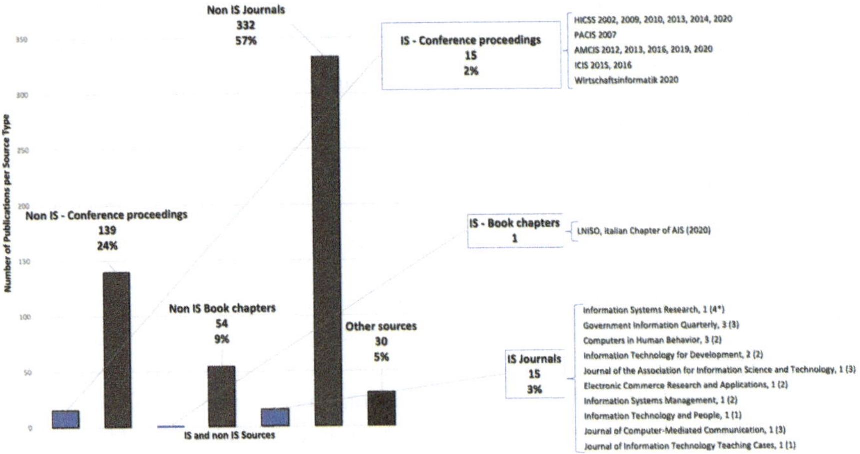

Fig. 2.3 Distribution of Publications among sources related to AIS and AJG2021 rank, and non-IS outlets

[1] https://aisel.aisnet.org/?AISeLibrary

[2] https://aisnet.org/page/SeniorScholarBasket

representing the only one among the top eight journals in IS. Finally, 15 publications are distributed in nine different ranked journals. Among the latter, the most prolific is *Government Information Quarterly* and *Computer in Human Behaviour*, with three publications each, classified as 3 and 2 in the AJG2021, respectively. Figure 2.3 summarizes the analysis by including the names of the sources, the journals and articles published, and their respective rank in the AJG. Next, the most productive countries are examined.

Figure 2.4 shows the number of contributions for each country based on the affiliation of the authors included in the dataset. Moreover, the graph distinguishes the publications whose authors belong to a single country (SCP) or multiple countries (MCP). In other words, it is also possible to identify the countries whose authors usually publish by collaborating with colleagues from different countries. The DT debate in NPOs has been significantly developed in the USA with 157 contributions, followed by the UK and Germany with significantly fewer publications (approximately 10% of the first country). However, although Spain is the second most productive country in the SCP category (13 publications), it is inactive in international collaborations (MCP) along with India, Brazil, Japan, Singapore, Sweden, Greece, Iran, and Poland.

Afterward, the analysis focused on the authors' production over time, considering the authors with at least three publications in the corpus. Figure 2.5 shows the 14 most productive authors over time. The dot size represents the number of published articles, while the intensity of the color defines the total citations per year.

Considering the number of papers contributed, Ferrucci P. is the most productive author, with eight articles published in different journals between 2015 and 2019. Campbell J. and Riggs C. follow with four contributions, respectively, between 2013–2017 and 2004–2007. The remaining authors contributed with three

Fig. 2.4 Most productive countries

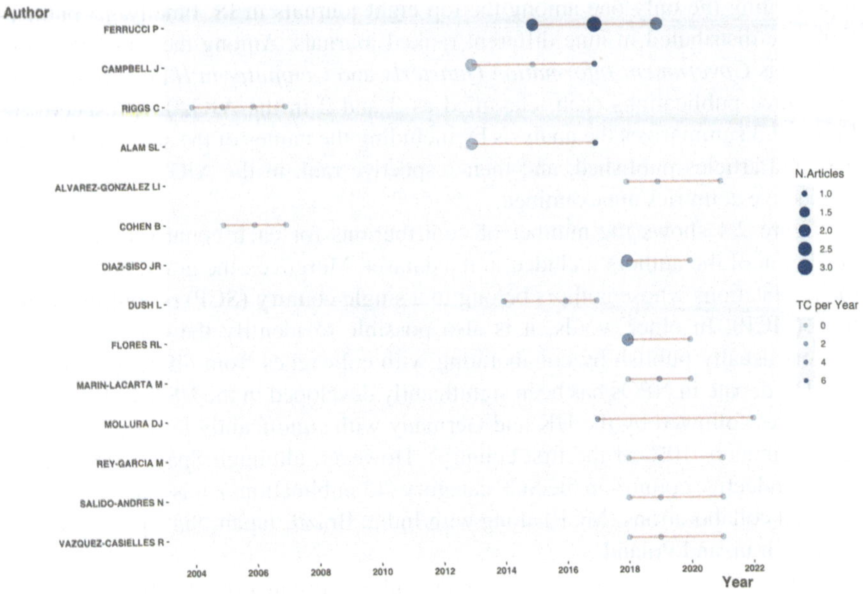

Fig. 2.5 The 14 most productive authors over time

publications, especially between 2017 and 2022, except for Cohen B, who contributed between 2005 and 2007. Regarding these authors' impact on literature, Ferrucci P. received a total of 111 citations, followed by Campbell J. and Alam S.L., with 38 citations overall. Finally, Dush L., Diaz-Siso J.R., Flores R.L., and Mollura D.J. received 20, 15, 15, and 14 citations, respectively. Notably, this result further confirms the growing interest in the DT discourse in NPOs over the last 4 years.

To further explore the contributions that have received more attention among scholars, especially concerning the IS field, a preliminary citation analysis is proposed (Baier-Fuentes et al., 2019; Merigó et al., 2015; Za & Braccini, 2017; Za, Pallud, et al., 2020b). Table 2.3 reports the 14 most cited papers collecting more than 50 citations. None of the three most prolific authors over time (Ferrucci P., Campbell J., and Riggs C.) appear in the top 25 best-cited papers. However, the most significant number of citations received by Ferrucci P. is 32 for his publication on *Journalism* (Ferrucci, 2015), followed by Campbell with 31 citations for his publication on the *Information Systems Research* journal (Alam & Campbell, 2017).

Also, it appears that Riggs C. has not yet received any citations. In comparison, Table 2.3 shows that Bakir and McStay (2018), who published on *Digital Journalism*, received 272 citations, representing the author receiving the highest number of citations. It is also interesting to note that Remané et al. (2017) is assigned 65 citations, representing the author receiving the highest number of citations as a publication in IS (i.e., representing a conference proceeding of ICIS2016).

Table 2.3 Top 13 most cited papers with at least 50 citations

Paper	TC	TCperY.
Bakir V., 2018, Digit Journal	272	54.40
Michelini L., 2018, Ecol Econ	93	18.60
Bendea H., 2008, Int Arch Photogram, Remote Sens Spat Inf Sci - Isprs Arch	83	5.53
Kim Y.M., 2018, Polit Commun	81	16.20
Bakker P., 2012, Journal Practice	76	6.90
Starbird K., 2013, Proc Acm Conf Comput Support Coop Work Cscw	75	7.50
Remane G., 2016, Int Conf Inf Syst, Icis	65	9.28
Voida A., 2011, Conf Hum Fact Comput Syst Proc	65	5.41
Wilson M.W., 2011, Soc Cult Geogr	64	5.33
Nee R.C., 2013, Jmm Int J Media Manage	63	6.30
Alberti F.G., 2017, J Bus Strategy	56	9.33
Le Dantec C.A., 2008, Proc Acm Conf Comput Support Coop Work Cscw	54	3.60
Kauffman R.J., 2012, Elect Commer Res Appl	50	4.54

Science Mapping Analysis

To investigate the most important topics regarding the DT discussions in NPOs, an analysis was conducted on the most frequently used keywords by authors. Specifically, an analysis of the frequency of keywords used by the authors is developed to investigate the relationship between the documents and their respective contributions to the debate. First, the trend of the top 41 most widely used keywords is examined. Then, by computing the co-word analysis, a thematic map is developed, identifying keyword clusters based on their centrality and density measures.

The scatter plot in Fig. 2.6 shows the thematic trend chart based on time (years are on the x-axis) and terms (keywords are on the y-axis). Specifically, the reference year for each term is identified using the median of the distribution of occurrences from 1994 to 2021 (automatically established by considering an acceptance threshold set at a minimum of eight occurrences for an author's keyword). Consequently, for each year, it is possible to recognize the terms in descending order of frequency (Aria & Cuccurullo, 2017). Additionally, for each keyword, the size of the sphere is proportional to the total number of its occurrences. At the same time, the line represents the specific period during which authors used that keyword.

Among 1808 different keywords used in the documents in the dataset, 41 meet the predefined occurrence threshold. The frequency of the 41 keywords, in line with the trend of publications, increases significantly between 2016 and 2021, with a lower level in 2014. Specifically, this initial period, including the term "digital transformation" (42 occurrences, third most frequent), shows a higher and more

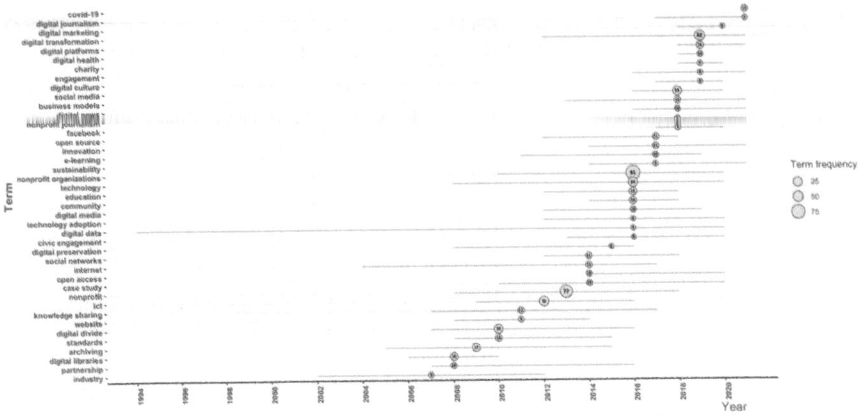

Fig. 2.6 Top 41 keywords used by authors in and their trends over the years

concentrated level of occurrences concerning multidisciplinary topics related to DT and NPOs. Some frequent keywords are *COVID-19*, *digital platform*, *digital health*, *business models*, and *charity*, representing the concepts associated with discussions that include the theme of the pandemic. It is not surprising that authors have used these keywords, considering the various challenges arising from the pandemic (this is logically inferred considering the prevailing engagement of NPOs in social functions, and the reference period 2020–2022). In comparison, keywords like "nonprofit" (77 occurrences), *knowledge sharing*, *ICT*, and *digital libraries* have been used more frequently after 2002. The latter seems to represent an early period when researchers began to analyze the impact of technology on NPOs. Considering "nonprofit organizations," another period appears to refer to studies exploring the development and adoption of digitized channels in NPOs, where typical keywords are *community*, *digital media*, *social networks*, and the *internet*. Interestingly, "digital data" is the authors' keyword covering the most extended period (from 1994 to 2020), with the median of its distribution in 2016.

The following step involves computing the co-occurrence of keywords (Callon et al., 1991; Cobo et al., 2011; Zupic & Čater, 2015) to develop a thematic map afterwards. This preliminary analysis serves to investigate the relationships among the primary topics discussed within the dataset. Specifically, it aims to identify how frequently each keyword appears in conjunction with others (Aria & Cuccurullo, 2017). Then it provides the groundwork for an examination of the evolution of the terminology, which is eventually considered for examining and representing the most significant themes in the discussion on DT in NPOs.

Hence, starting from the co-occurrence network of all keywords, a thematic map is developed by calculating the centrality and density of each cluster (Cobo et al., 2011). Following Cobo et al. (2011), the thematic map consists of an in-depth analysis of the important topics discussed in a dataset (Callon et al., 1991; Cobo et al., 2011; Zupic & Čater, 2015). Specifically, the thematic map helps identify clusters (research themes) of keywords based on the strength of their interconnections. For this analysis, the "simple centers algorithm" was employed (Cobo et al., 2011) during calculation, obtaining results and a graphical representation (see Fig. 2.7). Moreover, in the thematic map, the clusters are shown according to their density and centrality measures. The density is an indicator of the general level of connectedness of the graph (internal connections between the keywords belonging to the same cluster). The centrality defines the number of ties given to a node (the external connection between different clusters). Hence, density represents the development of topics (themes), while centrality represents the relevance of topics (themes) for the entire research domain. Notably, the centrality is assigned to the x-axis, while the density is assigned to the y-axis. Accordingly, considering the combination of high and low values for the two parameters, it is possible to define such a strategic diagram composed of four categories of themes. That is, the *motor themes*, which are well-established and theoretically relevant (high centrality, high density). The *niche themes* are highly developed and isolated (low centrality, high density). The *emerging or declining themes* that are weakly or marginally developed (low centrality, low density). Finally, the *basic and transversal themes* are theoretically relevant but poorly developed (high centrality, low density). Figure 2.7 depicts the thematic map, which outlines the themes concerning each cluster and summarizes the discussion regarding the DT debate in NPOs. Hereafter, each quadrant of the thematic map is described in relation to the clusters assigned to them and the keywords contributing to the definition of the cluster, with their frequency in parentheses.

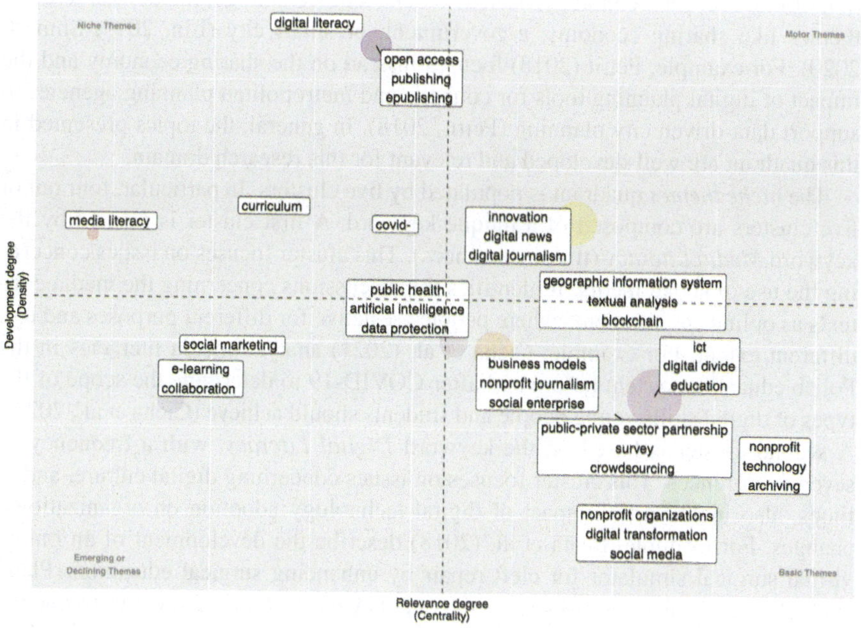

Fig. 2.7 Thematic map based on the most recurring authors' keywords

The *motor themes* quadrant consists of one well-placed cluster and another on edge with the *basic themes* quadrant. The former cluster, with a frequency of 52 occurrences, includes the keywords *Innovation* (11), *Digital News* (10), *Digital Journalism* (8), *Journalism* (7), *Public Journalism* (6), *Entrepreneurial Journalism* (5), and *Network* (5). It recognizes one of the most discussed topics concerning DT in NPOs over the last 5 years: the impact of digital technologies on the production of nonprofit news and nonprofit journalism. For example, Buschow and Suhr (2022) conduct a case study to analyze a novel organization, a nonprofit startup in Germany, that differs considerably from traditional media firms in terms of its functional roles and organizational practices of media work (Buschow & Suhr, 2022). Bodrozic and Paulussen (2018) investigate a nonprofit digital media startup that aims to create a space for Muslims and non-Muslims in Belgium (Bodrozic & Paulussen, 2018). The second cluster includes the following keywords with their occurrences: *Geographic Information System* (7), *Textual Analysis* (5), *Blockchain* (5), *Smart City* (5), and *Sharing Economy* (5). This cluster is not well-positioned in a quadrant as it includes different discussions regarding recent and poorly debated technology and other well-established and debated ones. Specifically, it seems that geographic information systems represent a motor theme as it is a well-established topic in the literature concerning NPOs (Cipriano & Za, 2021; McNutt et al., 2018; Zukin, 2020). For example, Mitchell and Elwood (2012) discuss the integration of local history and geography through collaborative digital mapping for improving civic participation by early adolescent learners (Mitchell & Elwood, 2012). Instead, some basic and transversal themes are represented by discussions concerning the adoption of more recent technology, such as blockchain technology, in addition to other themes like sharing economy, e-government, or smart city (Lin, 2019; Shmidt, 2020). For example, Pettit (2018) focuses instead on the sharing economy and the impact of digital planning tools for councils and metropolitan planning agencies to support data-driven city planning (Pettit, 2018). In general, the topics presented in this quadrant are well-developed and relevant for this research domain.

The *niche themes* quadrant is populated by five clusters. In particular, four out of five clusters are composed of a unique keyword. A first cluster is formed by the keyword *Media Literacy* (five occurrences). This cluster focuses on issues concerning the use of social media. It identifies the discussions concerning the media contexts as online environments where people are active for different purposes and to a different extent. For example, Cicha et al. (2021) analyze media literacies in the Polish education system before and after COVID-19 to determine the scope of the types of digital skills young people and students should achieve (Cicha et al., 2021). A second cluster is based on the keyword *Digital Literacy*, with a frequency of seven occurrences. This cluster focuses on issues concerning digital culture, and at times, also includes the impact of digital technology adoption on organizational changes. For example, Plana et al. (2018) describe the development of an online virtual surgical simulator for cleft repair by enhancing surgical education (Plana et al., 2018). A third cluster includes the only keyword *COVID-19*, with a frequency of 13 occurrences. This cluster represents the discussions concerning the involvement of NPOs in response to the issues triggered by the COVID-19 pandemic. For example, Ebrahimigharehbaghi et al. (2022) explore nonprofit crisis management in Ireland, considering how the organization responded and adapted its service offering (Ebrahimigharehbaghi et al., 2022). Also, Ravi et al. (2021) investigate some education settings in India involved in the transition of workflows to digital platforms due to the pandemic. In particular, these authors analyze some underserved contexts with limited, intermittent, and shared access to mobile or computing devices and the internet (Ravi et al., 2021). A fourth cluster is based on the keyword *Curriculum* (five occurrences). This cluster represents the debate concerning curriculum, whether in designing specific or digital skills, courses, and teaching activities involving different stakeholders. In this regard, Astrachan and Osborne (2016) describe a project intended to broaden participation in computer science in high school and support teachers with limited previous experience (Astrachan & Osborne, 2016). Finally, a fifth cluster has a frequency of 21 occurrences. This cluster includes the keywords *Open Access* (10), *Publishing* (6), and *Epublishing* (5). It focuses on the discussions concerning epublishing about the issues characterizing the open access of sources, for-profit, public, and nonprofit perspectives, as well as the management of libraries and copyright. For example, Bruno and Amico (2020) describe different initiatives fostered by a specialized nonprofit library in Latin America during the COVID-19 pandemic (Bruno & Amico, 2020). Overall, the topics presented in this quadrant, as highly developed and isolated, seem to be representative of some discussions drawing the commitment of some NPOs to developing DT initiatives in response to the challenges triggered by COVID-19 (Ameli et al., 2022; d'Orville, 2020; Obradović et al., 2021; Rapanta et al., 2021).

The *emerging or declining* themes quadrant is composed of two clusters. By examining those clusters and considering the results of previous qualitative studies, such clusters seem to recognize emerging discussions, given the variety of NPOs, their resource availability, and the diversity of social services they offer (Henriksen et al., 2012; Jeong & Cui, 2020). A first cluster includes the keywords *E-learning* (10) and *Collaboration* (5). Analyzing the content of the papers in this cluster, it particularly appears that some discussions are further related to the challenges triggered by COVID-19. For example, Schulte et al. (2021) focus on the digitalization in medical education during COVID-19 and report that although the tool adequately meets the demand, it cannot replace human interaction (Schulte et al., 2021). Zhao et al. (2019) analyze an open online platform introducing massive online learning into health emergency response. Specifically, these authors seek to understand the pattern of distribution that facilitates improved platform reach, investigating the operational model of nonprofit platforms (Zhao et al., 2019). In comparison, a second cluster is represented by the keyword *Social Marketing* (five occurrences). This cluster represents the discussion on diverse initiatives concerning digital technology adoption, enabling marketing purposes and the organizational and societal implications related to social marketing (representing an emerging theme). Irfan and Salam (2020) analyze a nonprofit digital literacy training for rural women entrepreneurs for developing an e-commerce platform to sell handicrafts (Irfan & Salam, 2020).

Finally, the *basic and transversal themes* quadrant is populated by six clusters. Keywords with high centrality and low density characterize these clusters. Thus, they include theoretically relevant topics but are little developed since they present a robust external connection between different clusters and a limited internal relationship among the keywords belonging to the same cluster. This is evident by considering the various authors' keywords and related co-occurrences populating the clusters of such a quadrant. In addition, as basic themes, it is unsurprisingly noticed that most of the discussions representing these clusters are also discussed in the literature, without examining DT. Hence, for this quadrant, except for one specific cluster deserving more attention, only the major relevant aspects of the clusters and related topics are highlighted after a short presentation of each cluster, its representative keywords, and associated frequencies. However, these clusters represent further opportunities to enrich the debate by investigating the internal relationship among the keywords belonging to each cluster. A first particular cluster includes the keywords *Public Health* (6), *Artificial Intelligence* (6), and *Data Protection* (5). Interestingly, such a cluster partially overlaps with the emerging or declining themes quadrant. That is, it focuses on discussions exploring public health (a basic theme), at times, also concerning the adoption of more recent digital technologies (where the keywords *Artificial Intelligence* and *Data Protection* represent emerging aspects with respect to previous studies). For example, McKillop et al. (2021) explore how an information system designed for social programs helps deliver services effectively and efficiently across diverse programs (McKillop et al., 2021). Remarkably, they notice some important aspects for digital transformation and organizational changes, such as secure information sharing and collaboration through data standardization and aggregation (McKillop et al., 2021). Afterward, the second cluster includes the keywords *Nonprofit Organizations* (91), *Digital Transformation* (42), *Social Media* (33), *Digital Platforms* (15), *Community* (14), *Social Networks* (11), *Digital Media* (10), *Charity* (9), *Facebook* (9), and *Website* (9). The third cluster includes the keywords *Public–Private Sector Partnership* (6), *Survey* (6), and *Crowdsourcing* (5). The fourth contains the keywords ICT (36), *Digital Divide* (30), *Education* (16), *Internet* (11), *Technology Adoption* (8), *E-government* (7), *Educational Technology* (6), *Homeless* (6), *Digital Communication* (5), and *Digital Inequality* (5). The fifth cluster includes the keywords *Nonprofit* (77), *Technology* (34), *Archiving* (17), *Digital Libraries* (16), *Standards* (13), *Knowledge Sharing* (11), *Open Source* (11), *Digital Health* (10), *Partnership* (10), and *Case Study* (10). Finally, the sixth cluster includes the keywords *Business Models* (13), *Nonprofit Journalism* (9), *Social Enterprise* (6), *Analytics* (6), and *Business Ventures* (5). Therefore, the keywords of these six clusters outline some basic themes that confirm the results of previous research (Cipriano & Za, 2021, 2022a, 2022b). These themes are important for the research domain, and they could be applied to different research areas. It appears that various organizations are involved in the DT discussion, together with some NPOs. Other explicit partnerships or collaborations (Cipriano & Za, 2021, 2022a, 2022b), such as business ventures (Joghee, 2021) and social enterprises (Pawliczek et al., 2021), are here detected. This aspect further highlights the need for some NPOs to transform their organizational form to preserve their financial sustainability for accomplishing their social missions (Chang et al., 2021). Overall, this analysis shows that the debate is active mainly in three areas, presumably increased due to the challenges triggered by the COVID-19 pandemic. One area concerns digital channels, including the digitalization of communications and interactions at different levels and extents (Ihm & Lee, 2021; Uzcanga & Oiarzabal, 2019), further introducing analytics (McKillop et al., 2021) and IoT technology (Joghee, 2021). A second area concerns education, whether in terms of ability and competencies in using digital tools, as well as in enabling digitalized teaching, courses, lessons, training, and sharing of knowledge (Ndasi et al., 2021). Finally, a third area concerns the social aspect, such as the digital divide, digital inclusion, digital health, crowdfunding, homeless care, charity, and digital security (Van Winkle et al., 2019).

2.5 Final Considerations

This study provides a bibliometric analysis to examine the evolutionary trend of the DT discourse in NPOs. Based on 586 contributions, a performance analysis and a science mapping analysis have been proposed. The descriptive analysis depicts the growing interest in research on DT in NPOs. A significant impact is assigned to the last 4 years, with approximately 50% of the overall contributions. Then, the analysis focused on the 41 most frequent keywords and the co-occurrences of all the authors' keywords to recognize thematic clusters. Accordingly, the focus moved to the thematic map to describe the topics (representing themes), summarizing the overall discourse. As a result, multiple research themes related to the specific context of NPOs emerged, providing insights concerning the evolution of such themes, their relevance, and relations. Some novel discussions based on the different allocations of the themes in the thematic map were then progressed, recognizing also some recurring topics that confirm the results of previous qualitative studies, while highlighting new themes. For example, this study presented other forms of collaboration or partnerships among different organizations in addition to NPOs (Joghee, 2021; Pawliczek et al., 2021). Also, it was noticed that some papers discussed the (IoT) technology, or analytics and their use (Joghee, 2021; McKillop et al., 2021). Then, three main areas of investigation that seem significant but not strongly developed yet (considering the mutual analysis of all the keywords of a cluster) were inferred. Those areas are concerning digital communications, digital education, and digital society (as a representative label to recognize the relevance given to some civil and social aspects). Moreover, the different analyses showed that concerning NPOs the DT debate has been affected significantly concerning the need to manage uncertainty and unexpected events triggered by the COVID-19 pandemic (Hai et al., 2021; Nagel, 2020).

To complement such a conceptual synthesis, a summary of the main themes related to such an academic debate is provided to conclude. By further developing the review and integrating the conceptual results related to Figs. 2.6 and 2.7, the rationale is now to show how the identified three main thematic areas (digital communication, digital education, and digital society) group concepts (represented by keywords) regardless of the period in which they were used. Observing Fig. 2.6, it can be noted that the keywords with the most occurrences, which are nonprofit (77), nonprofit organizations (91), and digital transformation (42), could also represent three distinct periods outlining the presence and evolution of different discussions. At the same time, assumptions develop on the thematic map, where the clusters group the different concepts (given also the co-occurrences among authors' keywords), representing a different evolution and presence of related themes (representative discussions in the literature). All in all, considering the concepts grouped in the different clusters of the thematic map, and the placement of the different authors' keywords on the temporal axis (x-axis in Fig. 2.6), one can recognize some keywords (as themes) representing the three thematic areas over time. Table 2.4 provides the analytical details of this insight.

These results could support the many stakeholders interested in exploring the most important publications and the terminology related to DT in NPOs in greater depth from a longitudinal perspective. This review can assist other researchers in identifying relevant themes and concepts, selecting specific keywords for further research, and including any publications that use related terms.

As a contribution, this research investigated the scientific production related to the primary sources of the IS community. As a result, the IS community seems to pay limited attention to the DT debate in NPOs due to the limited number of studies published in sources belonging to such a domain. Moreover, this review could support further researchers in developing additional studies concerning DT in NPOs.

Finally, this study has some limitations. First, this research is based only on Scopus and does not use other databases to integrate the corpus. Second, it focused on the co-word analysis, providing a preliminary citation analysis. So, in a future step, a complete citation and co-citation analysis could be performed to describe the evolution of topics about citation patterns and recognize co-citation networks and different communities. For example, the multiple correspondence analysis (MCA) could be used to investigate the relationship between the keywords and citations. Third, since this research primarily relies on the analysis of the authors' keywords, it could be helpful to perform a computational literature review as a complementary approach for integrating the analysis of the abstracts of the corpus. Moreover, as a

Table 2.4 The thematic areas over time (given the trend of authors' keywords)

	Thematic area		
Representative keywords—period	*Digital Communication*	*Digital Education*	*Digital Society*
Nonprofit (2002–2020)	Digital data Knowledge sharing	Archiving E-learning	Industry Digital health
Nonprofit Organizations (1994–2020)	Internet Social media	Digital culture Education	Community Civic engagement
Digital Transformation (2011–2022)	Social networks Digital media	Open access Digital journalism	Covid-19 Engagement

further step, further investigations could also consider examining if the contributions assigned to a cluster are mainly published in journal articles, conference proceedings, or book chapters, further recognizing the relevance and novelty of a topic.

References

Adekunle, S. A., Aigbavboa, C. O., Ejohwomu, O., Adekunle, E. A., & Thwala, W. D. (2021). Digital transformation in the construction industry: A bibliometric review. *Journal of Engineering, Design and Technology*. https://doi.org/10.1108/JEDT-08-2021-0442

Alam, S. L., & Campbell, J. (2017). Temporal motivations of volunteers to participate in cultural crowdsourcing work. *Information Systems Research, 28*(4), 744–759. https://doi.org/10.1287/isre.2017.0719

Ali, M. F. (2022). Between panic and motivation: Did the first wave of COVID-19 affect scientific publishing in Mediterranean countries? *Scientometrics*, 0123456789. https://doi.org/10.1007/s11192-022-04391-w

Ameli, M., Shams Esfandabadi, Z., Sadeghi, S., Ranjbari, M., & Zanetti, M. C. (2022). COVID-19 and Sustainable Development Goals (SDGs): Scenario analysis through fuzzy cognitive map modeling. *Gondwana Research*, xxxx. https://doi.org/10.1016/j.gr.2021.12.014

Aria, M., & Cuccurullo, C. (2017). Bibliometrix: An R-tool for comprehensive science mapping analysis. *Journal of Informetrics, 11*(4), 959–975. https://doi.org/10.1016/j.joi.2017.08.007

Aria, M., & Cuccurullo, C. (2022). Comprehensive science mapping analysis. *Package "Bibliometrix"*.

Aria, M., Cuccurullo, C., D'Aniello, L., Misuraca, M., & Spano, M. (2022). Thematic analysis as a new culturomic tool: The social media coverage on COVID-19 pandemic in Italy. *Sustainability, 14*(6), 3643. https://doi.org/10.3390/su14063643

Aria, M., Misuraca, M., & Spano, M. (2020). Mapping the evolution of social research and data science on 30 years of social indicators research. *Social Indicators Research, 149*(3), 803–831. https://doi.org/10.1007/s11205-020-02281-3

Astrachan, O., & Osborne, R. B. (2016). Advanced placement computer science principles (APCSP): A report from teachers. *Proceedings of the 47th ACM technical symposium on computer science education (SIGCSE '16)*, 681–682.

Baier-Fuentes, H., Merigó, J. M., Amorós, J. E., & Gaviria-Marín, M. (2019). International entrepreneurship: A bibliometric overview. *International Entrepreneurship and Management Journal, 15*(2), 385–429. https://doi.org/10.1007/s11365-017-0487-y

Baiyere, A., Grover, V., Lyytinen, K. J., Woerner, S., & Gupta, A. (2023). Digital "x"—Charting a path for digital-themed research. *Information Systems Research, 34*(2), 463–486. https://doi.org/10.1287/isre.2022.1186

Baiyere, A., Mosconi, E., Wessel, L., & Indulska, M. (2022). Frontiers in digital transformation research. *Information Systems Journal*.

Bakir, V., & McStay, A. (2018). Fake news and the economy of emotions. *Digital Journalism, 6*(2), 154–175. https://doi.org/10.1080/21670811.2017.1345645

Bekkers, R., & Wiepking, P. (2011). A literature review of empirical studies of philanthropy: Eight mechanisms that drive charitable giving. *Nonprofit and Voluntary Sector Quarterly, 40*(5), 924–973. https://doi.org/10.1177/0899764010380927

Benbunan-Fich, R., Desouza, K. C., & Andersen, K. N. (2020). IT-enabled innovation in the public sector: Introduction to the special issue. *European Journal of Information Systems, 29*(4), 323–328. https://doi.org/10.1080/0960085X.2020.1814989

Bharadwaj, A., El Sawy, O. A., Pavlou, P. A., & Venkatraman, N. (2013). Digital business strategy: Toward a next generation of insights. *MIS Quarterly, 37*(2), 471–482. https://doi.org/10.25300/MISQ/2013/37:2.3

Bodrozic, S., & Paulussen, S. (2018). Citizen media practices at the digital startup Mvslim. *Journalism Practice, 12*(8), 1061–1069. https://doi.org/10.1080/17512786.2018.1493945

Börner, K., Chen, C., & Boyack, K. W. (2005). Visualizing knowledge domains. *Annual Review of Information Science and Technology, 37*(1), 179–255. https://doi.org/10.1002/aris.1440370106

Bracarense, N., Bawack, R., Wamba, S. F., & Carillo, K. D. A. (2022). Artificial intelligence and sustainability: A bibliometric analysis and future research directions. *Pacific Asia Journal of the Association for Information Systems, 14*(2), 136–159. https://doi.org/10.17705/1pais.14209

Brink, H., Packmohr, S., & Vogelsang, K. (2020). Fields of action to advance the digital transformation of NPOs—Development of a framework. In *Lecture notes in business information processing* (Vol. 398 LNBIP, pp. 82–97). https://doi.org/10.1007/978-3-030-61140-8_6

Bruno, P., & Amico, D. (2020). COVID-19 at Biblioteca Utopía, Buenos Aires, Argentina. https://doi.org/10.1080/10572317.2020.1834252.

Buschow, C., & Suhr, M. (2022). Change management and new organizational forms of content creation. In *Media and change management* (pp. 381–397). Springer International Publishing. https://doi.org/10.1007/978-3-030-86680-8_21

Callon, M., Courtial, J. P., & Laville, F. (1991). Co-word analysis as a tool for describing the network of interactions between basic and technological research: The case of polymer chemsitry. *Scientometrics, 22*(1), 155–205. https://doi.org/10.1007/BF02019280

Caputo, A., Marzi, G., Maley, J., & Silic, M. (2019). Ten years of conflict management research 2007-2017. *International Journal of Conflict Management, 30*(1), 87–110. https://doi.org/10.1108/IJCMA-06-2018-0078

Carroll, N. (2020). Theorizing on the normalization of digital transformations. In *Twenty-eighth European conference on information systems (ECIS) - A virtual AIS conference.*

Carroll, N., Hassan, N. R., Junglas, I., Hess, T., & Morgan, L. (2023). Transform or be transformed: The importance of research on managing and sustaining digital transformations. *European Journal of Information Systems, 32*(3), 347–353. https://doi.org/10.1080/0960085X.2023.2187033

Castriotta, M., Loi, M., Marku, E., & Naitana, L. (2019). What's in a name? Exploring the conceptual structure of emerging organizations. *Scientometrics, 118*(2), 407–437. https://doi.org/10.1007/s11192-018-2977-2

Chang, Y., Peng, X.-E., & Liang, C. (2021). Transforming nonprofit organisations into social enterprises: An experience-based follow-up study. *Voluntas: International Journal of Voluntary and Nonprofit Organizations, 32*(1), 3–12. https://doi.org/10.1007/s11266-020-00261-2

Chanias, S., Myers, M. D., & Hess, T. (2019). Digital transformation strategy making in pre-digital organizations: The case of a financial services provider. *The Journal of Strategic Information Systems, 28*(1), 17–33. https://doi.org/10.1016/j.jsis.2018.11.003

Chawla, R. N., & Goyal, P. (2022). Emerging trends in digital transformation: A bibliometric analysis. *Benchmarking: An International Journal, 29*(4), 1069–1112. https://doi.org/10.1108/BIJ-01-2021-0009

Chinotaikul, P., & Vinayavekhin, S. (2020). Digital transformation in business and management research: Bibliometric and co-word network analysis. In *2020 1st international conference on big data analytics and practices (IBDAP)* (pp. 1–5). IEEE. https://doi.org/10.1109/IBDAP50342.2020.9245456

Cicha, K., Rizun, M., Rutecka, P., & Strzelecki, A. (2021). COVID-19 and higher education: First-year students' expectations toward distance learning. *Sustainability, 13*(4), 1889. https://doi.org/10.3390/su13041889

Cipriano, M., & Za, S. (2021). Exploring the discourse on digital transformation in the domain of non-profit organisations. In F. Ceci, A. Prencipe, & P. Spagnoletti (Eds.), *Exploring innovation in a digital world. Lecture notes in information systems and organisation* (Vol. 51, pp. 198–231). Springer. https://doi.org/10.1007/978-3-030-87842-9_15

Cipriano, M., & Za, S. (2022a). A cluster analysis for research on digital transformation in non-profit organisations. In *Thirtieth European conference on information systems (ECIS 2022),Timisoara, Romania* (p. 13). https://aisel.aisnet.org/ecis2022_rip/54

Cipriano, M., & Za, S. (2022b). Which digital transformation strategy for non-profit organisations non-profit organisations? In *Thirtieth European conference on information systems (ECIS 2022),Timisoara, Romania* (p. 19). https://aisel.aisnet.org/ecis2022_rp/153

Cipriano, M., & Za, S. (2025). Exploring the discourse on digital transformation in nonprofit organizations. *Information & Management, 62*(6), 104165. https://doi.org/10.1016/j.im.2025.104165

Cobo, M. J., Jürgens, B., Herrero-Solana, V., Martínez, M. A., & Herrera-Viedma, E. (2018). Industry 4.0: A perspective based on bibliometric analysis. *Procedia Computer Science, 139*, 364–371. https://doi.org/10.1016/j.procs.2018.10.278

Cobo, M. J., López-Herrera, A. G., Herrera-Viedma, E., & Herrera, F. (2011). An approach for detecting, quantifying, and visualizing the evolution of a research field: A practical application to the Fuzzy Sets Theory field. *Journal of Informetrics, 5*(1), 146–166. https://doi.org/10.1016/j.joi.2010.10.002

Currie, W., Hsu, C., Van Vliet, B., & Weerakkody, V. (2022). Digital transformation as geo--political, organizational and technological nexus. *Journal of Information Technology*.

de Bem Machado, A., Secinaro, S., Calandra, D., & Lanzalonga, F. (2022). Knowledge management and digital transformation for industry 4.0: A structured literature review. *Knowledge Management Research & Practice, 20*(2), 320–338. https://doi.org/10.1080/14778238.2021.2015261

Di Vaio, A., Hassan, R., & Palladino, R. (2023). Blockchain technology and gender equality: A systematic literature review. *International Journal of Information Management, 68*(April 2022), 102517. https://doi.org/10.1016/j.ijinfomgt.2022.102517

Donthu, N., Kumar, S., & Pattnaik, D. (2020). Forty-five years of Journal of Business Research: A bibliometric analysis. *Journal of Business Research, 109*, 1–14. https://doi.org/10.1016/j.jbusres.2019.10.039

d'Orville, H. (2020). COVID-19 causes unprecedented educational disruption: Is there a road towards a new normal? *Prospects, 49*(1–2), 11–15. https://doi.org/10.1007/s11125-020-09475-0

Ebrahimigharehbaghi, S., Qian, Q. K., De Vries, G., & Visscher, H. J. (2022). From collective to individual decision-making: Barriers and opportunities to improve the success rate of the energy retrofits in the Dutch owner-occupied sector. In *CLIMA 2022 - The 14th REHVA HVAC world congress* (pp. 1–8). https://doi.org/10.34641/clima.2022.3301

Ferreira, M. P., Santos, J. C., de Almeida, M. I. R., & Reis, N. R. (2014). Mergers & acquisitions research: A bibliometric study of top strategy and international business journals, 1980–2010. *Journal of Business Research, 67*(12), 2550–2558. https://doi.org/10.1016/j.jbusres.2014.03.015

Ferrucci, P. (2015). Public journalism no more: The digitally native news nonprofit and public service journalism. *Journalism, 16*(7), 904–919. https://doi.org/10.1177/1464884914549123

Gopal, R. D., Hidaji, H., Kutlu, S. N., Patterson, R. A., & Yaraghi, N. (2023). Law, economics, and privacy: Implications of government policies on website and third-party information sharing. *Information Systems Research*, (March), 1–23. https://doi.org/10.1287/isre.2022.1178

Hai, T. N., Van, Q. N., & Thi Tuyet, M. N. (2021). Digital transformation: Opportunities and challenges for leaders in the emerging countries in response to Covid-19 pandemic. *Emerging Science Journal, 5*(Special Issue), 21–36. https://doi.org/10.28991/esj-2021-SPER-03

Hanelt, A., Bohnsack, R., Marz, D., & Antunes Marante, C. (2021). A systematic review of the literature on digital transformation: Insights and implications for strategy and organizational change. *Journal of Management Studies, 58*(5), 1159–1197. https://doi.org/10.1111/joms.12639

Hansmann, H. B. (1981). In H. B. Hansmann (Ed.), *Reforming nonprofit corporation law* (Vol. 129).

Hausberg, J. P., Liere-Netheler, K., Packmohr, S., Pakura, S., & Vogelsang, K. (2019). Research streams on digital transformation from a holistic business perspective: A systematic literature review and citation network analysis. *Journal of Business Economics, 89*(8–9), 931–963. https://doi.org/10.1007/s11573-019-00956-z

Henriksen, L. S., Smith, S. R., & Zimmer, A. (2012). At the eve of convergence? Transformations of social service provision in Denmark, Germany, and the United States. *Voluntas: International*

Journal of Voluntary and Nonprofit Organizations, 23(2), 458–501. https://doi.org/10.1007/s11266-011-9221-5

Hess, T., Matt, C., Benlian, A., & Wiesböck, F. (2016). Options for formulating a digital transformation strategy. *MIS Quarterly Executive, 15*(2), 123–139. https://doi.org/10.1108/10878571211209314

Hofmann, S., Sæbø, Ø., Braccini, A. M., & Za, S. (2019). The public sector's roles in the sharing economy and the implications for public values. *Government Information Quarterly, 36*(4), 101399. https://doi.org/10.1016/j.giq.2019.101399

Huang, J.-H., Duan, X.-Y., He, F.-F., Wang, G.-J., & Hu, X.-Y. (2021). A historical review and Bibliometric analysis of research on Weak measurement research over the past decades based on Biblioshiny, 1–19.

Ihm, J., & Lee, S. (2021). How perceived costs and benefits of initial social media participation affect subsequent community-based participation. *Voluntas: International Journal of Voluntary and Nonprofit Organizations, 32*(6), 1320–1331. https://doi.org/10.1007/s11266-020-00200-1

Irfan, T., & Salam, M. T. (2020). Kaarvan Crafts Foundation: Embracing digital literacy for women empowerment. *Emerald Emerging Markets Case Studies, 10*(4), 1–34. https://doi.org/10.1108/EEMCS-06-2020-0215

Jeong, J., & Cui, T. S. (2020). The density of nonprofit organizations: Beyond community diversity and resource availability. *Voluntas: International Journal of Voluntary and Nonprofit Organizations, 31*(1), 213–226. https://doi.org/10.1007/s11266-019-00175-8

Joghee, S. (2021). Internet of Things-assisted E-marketing and distribution framework. *Soft Computing, 25*(18), 12291–12303. https://doi.org/10.1007/s00500-021-05920-0

Jöhnk, J., Ollig, P., Oesterle, S., & Riedel, L.-N. (2020). The complexity of digital transformation—Conceptualizing multiple concurrent initiatives. In *WI2020 Zentrale Tracks* (pp. 1051–1066). GITO Verlag. https://doi.org/10.30844/wi_2020_j8-joehnk

Kataeva, Z., Durrani, N., Izekenova, Z., & Rakhimzhanova, A. (2023). Evolution of gender research in the social sciences in post-Soviet countries: A bibliometric analysis. *Scientometrics*, 0123456789. https://doi.org/10.1007/s11192-022-04619-9

Kraus, S., Durst, S., Ferreira, J. J., Veiga, P., Kailer, N., & Weinmann, A. (2022). Digital transformation in business and management research: An overview of the current status quo. *International Journal of Information Management, 63*(August 2020), 102466. https://doi.org/10.1016/j.ijinfomgt.2021.102466

Kraus, S., Jones, P., Kailer, N., Weinmann, A., Chaparro-Banegas, N., & Roig-Tierno, N. (2021). Digital transformation: An overview of the current state of the art of research. *SAGE Open, 11*(3), 215824402110475. https://doi.org/10.1177/21582440211047576

Lamboglia, R., Lavorato, D., Scornavacca, E., & Za, S. (2021). Exploring the relationship between audit and technology. A bibliometric analysis. *Meditari Accountancy Research, 29*(5), 1233–1260. https://doi.org/10.1108/MEDAR-03-2020-0836

Legner, C., Eymann, T., Hess, T., Matt, C., Bo, T., Urbach, N., et al. (2017). Digitalisation: Opportunity and challenge for the business and information systems engineering community. *Business and Information Systems Engineering, 59*(4), 301–308. https://doi.org/10.1007/s12599-017-0484-2

Li, Y., Tan, B., Park, G., & Ha, E. (2022). Exploiting resource fluidity for digital transformation: A revelatory case study. In *43rd international conference on information systems (ICIS), Copenhagen, Denmark.*

Lin, Y. (2019). Government management model of non-profit organizations based on e-government. In *Proceedings of the 2019 7th international conference on computer and communications management* (pp. 164–168). ACM. https://doi.org/10.1145/3348445.3348464

Madon, S., & Schoemaker, E. (2021). Digital identity as a platform for improving refugee management. *Information Systems Journal, 31*(6), 929–953. https://doi.org/10.1111/isj.12353

Majchrzak, A., Lynne Markus, M., & Wareham, J. (2016). Designing for digital transformation: Lessons for information systems research from the study of ICT and societal challenges. *MIS Quarterly: Management Information Systems, 40*(2), 267–277. https://doi.org/10.25300/MISQ/2016/40

Markus, M. L., & Rowe, F. (2021). Guest editorial: Theories of digital transformation: A progress report. *Journal of the Association for Information Systems, 22*(2), 273–280. https://doi.org/10.17705/1jais.00661

Marzi, G., Caputo, A., Garces, E., & Dabic, M. (2020). A three decade mixed-method bibliometric investigation of the IEEE Transactions on Engineering Management. *IEEE Transactions on Engineering Management, 67*(1), 4–17. https://doi.org/10.1109/TEM.2018.2870648

Matt, C., Hess, T., & Benlian, A. (2015). Digital transformation strategies. *Business & Information Systems Engineering, 57*(5), 339–343. https://doi.org/10.1007/s12599-015-0401-5

McKillop, M., Snowdon, J., Willis, V. C., Alevy, S., Rizvi, R., Rewalt, K., et al. (2021). A system to support diverse social program management. *JMIR Medical Informatics, 9*(8), e23219. https://doi.org/10.2196/23219

McNutt, J., Guo, C., Goldkind, L., & An, S. (2018). Technology in nonprofit organizations and voluntary action. *Voluntaristics Review, 3*(1), 1–63. https://doi.org/10.1163/24054933-12340020

Merigó, J. M., Mas-Tur, A., Roig-Tierno, N., & Ribeiro-Soriano, D. (2015). A bibliometric overview of the Journal of Business Research between 1973 and 2014. *Journal of Business Research, 68*(12), 2645–2653. https://doi.org/10.1016/j.jbusres.2015.04.006

Mitchell, K., & Elwood, S. (2012). Mapping children's politics: The promise of articulation and the limits of nonrepresentational theory. *Environment and Planning D: Society and Space, 30*(5), 788–804. https://doi.org/10.1068/d9011

Monteiro, E., Constantinides, P., Scott, S., Shaikh, M., & Burton-Jones, A. (2022). Qualitative research methods in information systems: A call for phenomenon-focused problematization. *MIS Quarterly, 46*(4), i–xviii.

Munoz, A., Billsberry, J., & Ambrosini, V. (2022). Resilience, robustness, and antifragility: Towards an appreciation of distinct organizational responses to adversity. *International Journal of Management Reviews, 24*(2), 181–187. https://doi.org/10.1111/ijmr.12289

Munoz, A., Todres, M., & Rook, L. (2021). Empowering organisations to gain from uncertainty: A conceptualisation of antifragility through leveraging organisational routines in uncertain environments. *Australasian Business, Accounting and Finance Journal, 15*(3), 23–42. https://doi.org/10.14453/aabfj.v15i3.3

Nadkarni, S., & Prügl, R. (2021). Digital transformation: A review, synthesis and opportunities for future research. *Management Review Quarterly, 71*(2), 233–341. https://doi.org/10.1007/s11301-020-00185-7

Nagel, L. (2020). The influence of the COVID-19 pandemic on the digital transformation of work. *International Journal of Sociology and Social Policy, 40*(9/10), 861–875. https://doi.org/10.1108/IJSSP-07-2020-0323

Nahrkhalaji, S. S., Shafiee, S., Shafiee, M., & Hvam, L. (2019). Challenges of digital transformation: The case of the non-profit sector. In *Proceedings of 2018 IEEE international conference on industrial engineering and engineering management (IEEM)*. https://doi.org/10.1109/IEEM.2018.8607762

Ndasi, W., Bolat, E., & Roushan, G. (2021). Cause-related marketing advertising formats on nonprofit websites. *Journal of Advertising Research, 61*(3), 289–302. https://doi.org/10.2501/JAR-2021-012

Nicholson, B., Nielsen, P., & Saebo, J. (2021). Special issue: Digital platforms for development. *Information Systems Journal, 31*(6), 863–868. https://doi.org/10.1111/isj.12364

Nwankpa, J. K., & Roumani, Y. (2016). IT capability and digital transformation: A firm performance perspective. In *37th international conference on information systems* (pp. 1–16).

Obradović, T., Vlačić, B., & Dabić, M. (2021). Open innovation in the manufacturing industry: A review and research agenda. *Technovation, 102*, 102221. https://doi.org/10.1016/j.technovation.2021.102221

Pawliczek, A., Chlopecký, J., Oberreiterová, O., & Moravec, L. (2021). Havířov: "The City of Green" and Its Fourth Sector Sustainability Activities. One Case Study from the Czech Republic (pp. 171–211). https://doi.org/10.1007/978-3-030-75714-4_10.

Pee, L. G., Pan, S. L., Wang, J., & Wu, J. (2021). Designing for the future in the age of pandemics: A future-ready design research (FRDR) process. *European Journal of Information Systems, 30*(2), 157–175. https://doi.org/10.1080/0960085X.2020.1863751

Pettit, P. (2018). Three mistakes about doing good (and bad). *Journal of Applied Philosophy, 35*(1), 1–25. https://doi.org/10.1111/japp.12294

Pizzi, S., Venturelli, A., Variale, M., & Macario, G. P. (2021). Assessing the impacts of digital transformation on internal auditing: A bibliometric analysis. *Technology in Society, 67*(June), 101738. https://doi.org/10.1016/j.techsoc.2021.101738

Plana, J. C., Thavendiranathan, P., Bucciarelli-Ducci, C., & Lancellotti, P. (2018). Multimodality imaging in the assessment of cardiovascular toxicity in the cancer patient. *JACC: Cardiovascular Imaging, 11*(8), 1173–1186. https://doi.org/10.1016/j.jcmg.2018.06.003

Ponzoa, J. M., Gómez, A., & Mas, J. M. (2023). EU27 and USA institutions in the digital ecosystem: Proposal for a digital presence measurement index. *Journal of Business Research, 154*(2023), 113354. https://doi.org/10.1016/j.jbusres.2022.113354

Rahal, A., & Zainuba, M. (2019). The rating dilemma of academic management journals: Attuning the perceptions of peer rating. *Advances in Business Research, 9*, 26–45.

Rapanta, C., Botturi, L., Goodyear, P., Guàrdia, L., & Koole, M. (2021). Balancing technology, pedagogy and the new normal: Post-pandemic challenges for higher education. *Postdigital Science and Education, 3*(3), 715–742. https://doi.org/10.1007/s42438-021-00249-1

Ravi, P., Ismail, A., & Kumar, N. (2021). The pandemic shift to remote learning under resource constraints. *Proceedings of the ACM on Human-Computer Interaction, 5*(CSCW2), 1–28. https://doi.org/10.1145/3476055

Remané, G., Hanelt, A., Tesch, J. F., & Kolbe, L. M. (2017). In J. F. Tesch (Ed.), *Business model innovation in the era of the internet of things. Studies on the aspects of evaluation, decision making and tooling*. Springer. https://doi.org/10.1007/978-3-319-98723-1

Ricciardi, F., & Za, S. (2015). Smart city research as an interdisciplinary crossroads: A challenge for management and organization studies. In *Lecture notes in information systems and organisation* (Vol. 5, pp. 163–171). https://doi.org/10.1007/978-3-319-09450-2_14

Rowe, F. (2018). Being critical is good, but better with philosophy! From digital transformation and values to the future of IS research. *European Journal of Information Systems, 27*(3), 380–393. https://doi.org/10.1080/0960085X.2018.1471789

Salamon, L. M., & Sokolowski, S. W. (2016). Beyond nonprofits: Re-conceptualizing the third sector. *Voluntas: International Journal of Voluntary and Nonprofit Organizations, 27*(4), 1515–1545. https://doi.org/10.1007/s11266-016-9726-z

Schallmo, D., Williams, C. A., & Boardman, L. (2017). Digital transformation of business models - Best practice, enablers, and roadmap. *International Journal of Innovation Management, 21*(08). https://doi.org/10.1142/S136391961740014X

Schiliro, D. (2022). Digital economy and digital transformation. In *Digital technologies for entrepreneurship in industry 4.0* (pp. 26–42). IGI Global. https://doi.org/10.4018/978-1-6684-4265-4.ch002

Schulte, T. L., Gröning, T., Ramsauer, B., Weimann, J., Pin, M., Jerusalem, K., & Ridwan, S. (2021). Impact of COVID-19 on continuing medical education—Results of an online survey among users of a non-profit multi-specialty live online education platform. *Frontiers in Medicine, 8*(November), 1–10. https://doi.org/10.3389/fmed.2021.773806

Scornavacca, E., Paolone, F., Za, S., & Martiniello, L. (2020). Investigating the entrepreneurial perspective in smart city studies. *International Entrepreneurship and Management Journal, 16*, 1197. https://doi.org/10.1007/s11365-019-00630-4

Selander, L., & Jarvenpaa, S. L. (2016). Digital action repertoires and transforming a social movement organization. *MIS Quarterly, 40*(2), 331–352.

Shirish, A., Srivastava, S. C., & Panteli, N. (2023). Management and sustenance of digital transformations in the Irish microbusiness sector: Examining the key role of microbusiness owner-manager. *European Journal of Information Systems, 32*(3), 409–433. https://doi.org/10.1080/0960085X.2023.2166431

Shmidt, M. (2020). Participants' interaction with sharing economy platforms in Russia. *Information Technology & People, 33*(3), 897–917. https://doi.org/10.1108/ITP-10-2018-0443

Small, H. (1999). Visualizing science by citation mapping. *Journal of the American Society for Information Science, 50*(9), 799–813. https://doi.org/10.1002/(SICI)1097-4571(1999)50:9<799::AID-ASI9>3.0.CO;2-G

Taylor, R. (2010). Moving beyond empirical theory. In *Third sector research* (pp. 1–9). Springer. https://doi.org/10.1007/978-1-4419-5707-8_1

Tekic, Z., & Koroteev, D. (2019). From disruptively digital to proudly analog: A holistic typology of digital transformation strategies. *Business Horizons, 62*(6), 683–693. https://doi.org/10.1016/j.bushor.2019.07.002

Teubner, R. A. (2013). Information systems strategy: Theory, practice, and challenges for future research. *Business and Information Systems Engineering, 5*(4), 243–257. https://doi.org/10.1007/s12599-013-0279-z

Trischler, M. F. G., & Li-Ying, J. (2022). Exploring the relationship between multi-dimensional digital readiness and digital transformation outcomes. *International Journal of Innovation Management, 26*(03). https://doi.org/10.1142/S136391962240014X

Uzcanga, C., & Oiarzabal, P. J. (2019). Associations of migrants in Spain: An enquiry into their digital inclusion in the "network society" in the 2010s. *Voluntas: International Journal of Voluntary and Nonprofit Organizations, 30*(5), 947–961. https://doi.org/10.1007/s11266-019-00162-z

Van Winkle, B., Solad, Y., Vaswani, N., & Rosner, B. I. (2019). Navigating the digital health ecosystem to bridge the gap from innovation to transformation: A NODE. Health perspective on digital evidence. *Digital Biomarkers, 3*(2), 83–91. https://doi.org/10.1159/000500194

Verhoef, P. C., Broekhuizen, T., Bart, Y., Bhattacharya, A., Qi Dong, J., Fabian, N., & Haenlein, M. (2021). Digital transformation: A multidisciplinary reflection and research agenda. *Journal of Business Research, 122*, 889–901. https://doi.org/10.1016/j.jbusres.2019.09.022

Vial, G. (2019). Understanding digital transformation: A review and a research agenda. *Journal of Strategic Information Systems, 28*(2), 118–144. https://doi.org/10.1016/j.jsis.2019.01.003

Vogelsang, K., Packmohr, S., & Brink, H. (2021). Challenges of the digital transformation—Comparing nonprofit and industry organizations. In *Lecture notes in information systems and organisation* (Vol. 46, pp. 297–312). https://doi.org/10.1007/978-3-030-86790-4_21

vom Brocke, J., & Mendling, J. (2018). Frameworks for business process management: A taxonomy for business process management cases. In *Read* (pp. 1–17). https://doi.org/10.1007/978-3-319-58307-5_1

vom Brocke, J., Winter, R., Hevner, A., & Maedche, A. (2020). Special issue editorial—Accumulation and evolution of design knowledge in design science research: A journey through time and space. *Journal of the Association for Information Systems, 21*(3), 520–544. https://doi.org/10.17705/1jais.00611

Walker, J., & Wood, G. (2021). Methodology. Academic journal guide 2021. doi:https://doi.org/10.36548/jitdw.2021.2.

Warner, K. S. R., & Wäger, M. (2019). Building dynamic capabilities for digital transformation: An ongoing process of strategic renewal. *Long Range Planning, 52*(3), 326–349. https://doi.org/10.1016/j.lrp.2018.12.001

Weick, K. E., & Sutcliffe, K. M. (2015). In Wiley (Ed.), *Managing the unexpected: Sustained performance in a complex world* (3rd ed.). John Wiley & Sons.

Werle, M., & Laumer, S. (2022). Competitor identification: A review of use cases, data sources, and algorithms. *International Journal of Information Management, 65*(April), 102507. https://doi.org/10.1016/j.ijinfomgt.2022.102507

Wessel, L., Baiyere, A., Ologeanu-Taddei, R., Cha, J., & Blegind Jensen, T. (2021). Unpacking the difference between digital transformation and IT-enabled organizational transformation. *Journal of the Association for Information Systems, 22*(1), 102–129. https://doi.org/10.17705/1jais.00655

White, H. D., & McCain, K. W. (1998). Visualizing a discipline: An author co-citation analysis of information science, 1972–1995. *Journal of the American Society for Information Science, 49*(4), 327–355. https://doi.org/10.1002/(SICI)1097-4571(19980401)49:4<327::AID-ASI4>3.0.CO;2-W

Wiesböck, F., & Hess, T. (2020). Digital innovations. *Electronic Markets, 30*(1), 75–86. https://doi.org/10.1007/s12525-019-00364-9

Za, S., & Braccini, A. M. (2017). Tracing the roots of the organizational benefits of IT services. In *Exploring services science* (Vol. 279, pp. 3–11). https://doi.org/10.1007/978-3-319-56925-3_1

Za, S., Ghiringhelli, C., & Virili, F. (2020a). Organizational change and learning: An explorative bibliometric-based literature analysis. In *Lecture notes in information systems and organisation* (Vol. 33, pp. 429–442). https://doi.org/10.1007/978-3-030-23665-6_31

Za, S., Pallud, J., Agrifoglio, R., & Metallo, C. (2020b). Value co-creation in online communities: A preliminary literature analysis. In *Lecture notes in information systems and organisation* (Vol. 33, pp. 33–46). https://doi.org/10.1007/978-3-030-23665-6_4

Za, S., & Spagnoletti, P. (2013). Knowledge creation processes in information systems and management: Lessons from simulation studies. In *Lecture notes in information systems and organisation* (Vol. 2, pp. 191–204). https://doi.org/10.1007/978-3-642-37228-5_19

Zhao, Y., George, R., Utunen, H., & Gamhewage, G. (2019). OpenWHO traffic analysis: Can we predict non-profit course reach by dissemination channel? In *CEUR workshop proceedings* (pp. 261–266).

Zukin, S. (2020). Seeing like a city: How tech became urban. *Theory and Society, 49*(5–6), 941–964. https://doi.org/10.1007/s11186-020-09410-4

Zupic, I., & Čater, T. (2015). Bibliometric methods in management and organization. *Organizational Research Methods, 18*(3), 429–472. https://doi.org/10.1177/1094428114562629

Chapter 3
A Classification of the Debate

3.1 Conceptual Background

The study of digital transformation (DT) in nonprofit organizations (NPOs) remains a fragmented and understructured area within the broader DT literature. As outlined in Chap. 2, interest in this intersection has grown considerably in the midst of socio-technical and geopolitical shifts, particularly following the COVID-19 pandemic. Although there a growing number of contributions, little effort has been made to classify the nature of DT initiatives in NPOs systematically or to distil coherent patterns from the emerging literature.

This chapter addresses that gap by adopting a qualitative meta-synthesis approach (Cipriano & Za, 2024). Specifically, it aims to explore the academic discourse surrounding DT in NPOs in order to provide comprehension about how the literature conceptualizes and operationalizes this phenomenon across such an organizational context. The anticipated objective is twofold: first, to propose a taxonomy of DT initiatives in the nonprofit sector, capturing recurring themes, perspectives, and strategies; and second, to apply multivariate analysis techniques to uncover meaningful groupings or clusters within the literature, revealing underlying patterns in how DT is framed and studied.

Complementing the overview provided in Chap. 2 (focused on providing a broad bibliometric mapping of the field, highlighting volume, authorship, and high-level themes), the present chapter takes a more interpretive and inductive approach. Drawing solely from peer-reviewed journal articles, it focuses on the qualitative content of the literature, aiming to bring structure and typology to a previously diffuse conversation. This approach also lays the groundwork for the conceptual framework proposed in Chap. 4.

In so doing, this chapter supports the book's broader ambition to develop a coherent and empirically informed understanding of how DT is pursued, experienced, and evaluated within the nonprofit domain. The combination of taxonomy

M. Cipriano, *Digital Transformation in Non-profit Organizations*, SpringerBriefs in Information Systems,
https://doi.org/10.1007/978-3-032-20937-5_3

and clustering methods aims to clarify the current state of knowledge but also enable the identification of critical gaps and divergent logics across studies, and insights that will ultimately support both theoretical refinement and practical guidance for NPOs engaging with DT initiatives and related changes.

3.2 Research Design and Methodology

This chapter complements the broad bibliometric overview presented in Chap. 2 by undertaking a qualitative and structural synthesis of the literature on DT in NPOs. While the previous chapter mapped the field descriptively, identifying thematic concentrations and bibliographic trends, the present study is interpretive and inductive in orientation. It aims to reveal how DT is conceptualized, enacted, and framed within scholarly contributions, and to distil meaningful categories and patterns from a selected collection of scientific publications. To this aim, this research adopts a two-phase, mixed-method design integrating qualitative meta-synthesis (Cipriano & Za, 2024) with multivariate statistical analysis.

Based on recent developments in meta-synthesis methods in information systems (IS) research (Hoon, 2013; Skinner et al., 2022), the study is designed to summarize and structure the literature through the development of a taxonomy of the literature strictly discussing DT in NPOs. The anticipated taxonomy aims to identify a set of dimensions and values (i.e., categories) that reflect how scholars have theorized, observed, and narrated DT initiatives in the sector. To deepen the interpretive insights derived from this typology, the taxonomy is then used as categorical input for a cluster analysis (Cipriano & Za, 2025) using multiple correspondence analysis (MCA) (Le Roux & Rouanet, 2009) and hierarchical clustering on principal components (HCPC) (François Husson et al., 2010). These combined techniques enable the identification of latent profiles or "archetypes" within the academic discourse, offering an integrated view of the diversity and convergence in how DT is understood across such organizational and disciplinary settings.

The study follows an exploratory, iterative protocol by Nickerson et al.'s (2013) taxonomy development method and is framed within Venkatesh et al.'s (2013) "expansion" logic for mixed-methods research (Cipriano & Za, 2025). Specifically, the qualitative phase aims to inductively examine key characteristics and categories that define DT in NPOs. In contrast, the quantitative phase seeks to investigate associations among these characteristics and identify coherent groupings. The entire process is organized across four interrelated phases. A first phase of identification of the literature and definition of the corpus to be analyzed. The second phase concerns the inductive development of a taxonomy, based on an iterative coding and abstraction process. A third phase refers to the statistical clustering of the coded articles based on categorical variables derived from the taxonomy. Lastly, a fourth phase concerns the interpretation of emergent patterns, leading to the identification of archetypes and the basis for the conceptual framework advanced in Chap. 4.

A key principle guiding the entire process is to ensure mutual consistency between qualitative inductive insights and quantitative structural validation. That is, the taxonomy aims to represent a synthesized classification of what emerges from the literature, and the cluster analysis intends to provide an empirical assessment of how those ideas cluster across contributions. To summarize, this twofold approach is meant to bridge thematic fragmentation in the literature, concurrently positioning the empirical foundation for a strategic, theory-informed conceptualization of digital transformation in nonprofit organizations.

Dataset and Inclusion and Exclusion Criteria

As the basis for this meta-synthesis, the dataset was constructed through a transparent and replicable protocol, ensuring rigor and consistency in the selection of scientific contributions strictly focused on the analysis of DT initiatives in NPOs. The objective was to assemble a corpus of scholarly work that would allow for an in-depth qualitative study, followed by a quantitative classification of themes and patterns in the academic discourse.

To maximize the breadth and quality of the literature included, the Scopus database was used, as it offers extensive coverage of peer-reviewed journal articles across multiple disciplines relevant to DT and the nonprofit domain. Scopus was selected due to its indexing quality and disciplinary range, particularly in organizational studies, information systems, and social sciences (Baas et al., 2020; Pranckutė, 2021).

The search was designed to be inclusive and precise. To this end, the query combined exactly the key terms related to digital transformation and the nonprofit context, using the following terms: "digit*" AND "non-profit*". These terms were searched in the *title, abstract*, and *author keywords* fields. Boolean operators and wildcards were used to account for pluralization, regional spelling variants (e.g., "organisation" vs. "organization"), and grammatical inflections. Moreover, more generic terms related to technological aspects, such as "ICT," "information systems," or "IT," which were found to return a high volume of outdated or thematically irrelevant results, were deliberately excluded (i.e., considering they often skewed toward technical implementation without a structural or strategic transformation focus).

To ensure a high-quality and focused dataset, the inclusion criteria summarized in Table 3.1 were applied.

Titles and abstracts were screened manually by the researcher to assess thematic relevance. Articles that mentioned digitalization or nonprofit settings but did not intersect the two substantively (e.g., ICT for development, digital divides, or volunteer management without strategic DT framing) were excluded.

The initial search returned 261 documents. After applying the above criteria, including the removal of non-English documents and nonjournal publications, the dataset was reduced to 154 documents. A further thematic screening led to the

Table 3.1 Inclusion and exclusion criteria

Criterion	Description
Type of document	Only peer-reviewed journal articles were retained.
Language	Articles had to be published in English.
Publication type	Books, book chapters, conference papers, notes, short surveys, and reviews were excluded.
Relevance and thematic focus	Articles had to address changes or transformations in NPOs, including isolated functions like digital fundraising or marketing, or digital technology adoption. Only contributions that discussed structural, strategic, or organizational implications of digital technologies in NPOs were retained.

exclusion of 30 off-topic articles, resulting in a final set of 124 articles used for taxonomy development and subsequent analysis.

This dataset presents a publication range from 1983 to 2021, with a notable increase in publications observed after 2014, reflecting an accelerating interest in DT processes within NPOs, particularly after 2020, in combination with the year of dissemination of the COVID-19 pandemic. The distribution also highlights a multidisciplinary engagement with the topic, including several journals from social sciences and sector-specific publications.

Moreover, in terms of publications, the most representative journals include *Nonprofit and Voluntary Sector Quarterly*, *Voluntas*, and *Nonprofit Management and Leadership*. Despite the recent volume growth, the distribution of articles across fields underscores the lack of disciplinary consolidation in this area, an issue the current monograph seeks to address through structured synthesis. Among the journals publishing the retrieved documents, the final dataset reveals that only one publication is from the *Information Systems Research* journal, representing the IS disciplinary area. However, by combining an inclusive retrieval strategy with rigorous screening and a focus on conceptual relevance, this dataset offers a solid foundation for developing a nuanced taxonomy and revealing latent patterns in the DT discourse within the nonprofit sector.

3.3 Taxonomy Development Process

The taxonomy developed in this chapter serves as a foundational structure to classify and interpret the fragmented discourse surrounding DT discussions in NPOs (Cipriano & Za, 2025). It reflects an iterative and interpretive process grounded in both empirical insights and theoretical lenses, aligned with an established taxonomy development protocol (Kundisch et al., 2021; Kutzner et al., 2018; McKelvey, 1982; Remane et al., 2016). This process is the core component of the qualitative strand of this meta-synthesis and forms the analytical basis for the cluster analysis that follows. Through sequential cycles of analysis, a set of mutually exclusive dimensions and associated values that capture how the literature conceptualizes DT across organizational settings, strategic orientations, and technological domains was derived. Specifically, the taxonomy was developed through an iterative mixed-mode process, alternating between two complementary approaches of analysis. The *empirical-to-conceptual* approach builds dimensions and categories inductively from the data by closely reading and coding the selected articles (Nickerson et al., 2013). The *conceptual-to-empirical* approach draws on established theories and prior taxonomies to inform and refine the structure, ensuring theoretical alignment and extensibility (Nickerson et al., 2013).

This dual approach points to ensure groundedness in the literature and analytical coherence, aligning with the ending conditions proposed by Nickerson et al. (2013). That is, this iterative refinement aimed to produce a taxonomy that is *(i) concise*, avoiding redundancy and ambiguity; *(ii) comprehensive*, capturing the thematic variety of the field; *(iii) robust*, conceptually meaningful and logically consistent; *(iv) explanatory*, enabling interpretive insight into the discourse; and eventually *(v) extendible*, allowing for future inclusion of new categories (in the case of updates of the sample of analysis, or integration of the corpus including documents retrieved from different databases).

The taxonomy was finalized over five iterative cycles of analysis, each consisting of literature reviews, applying two analytical approaches to produce a result similar to the commonly known processes of *"open and axial coding,"* and systematic reassessment of dimensions and values. Specifically, the five cycles of analysis unfolded as follows:

1. Iteration (empirical). A preliminary coding of all 124 articles to inductively surface recurring patterns, leading to a first set of candidate dimensions.
2. Iteration (conceptual). Review of extant IS taxonomies (e.g., Knote et al., 2021; Bharadwaj et al., 2013) to evaluate conceptual overlaps and fill theoretical gaps. Initial dimensions included broad categories such as Focus, Typology, and Field.
3. Iteration (empirical). A second cycle of article classification revealed the need to shift from descriptive to strategic and organizational dimensions. New candidate dimensions reflecting DT characteristics in NPOs emerged.
4. Iteration (conceptual). Anchoring dimensions in theoretical frameworks on digital business strategy (Bharadwaj et al., 2013), digital innovation (Vial, 2019), and organizational change, we revised the dimensional structure to reflect DT as a sociotechnical phenomenon.
5. Iteration (empirical). Final calibration of values and dimension labels, validating exhaustiveness and mutual exclusivity through cross-coding, peer review, and a sample-based consistency check.

By performing this process, the researcher was able to develop a final taxonomy comprising 5 dimensions and 29 different values (categories for the following analysis), each representing a distinct analytical lens describing the discussions on DT in NPOs. The resulting five dimensions reflect both the substantive content of the articles and their strategic orientation, and are defined as follows:

- Digital scope. This dimension aims to capture the technological ambition and strategic intent of the DT initiative (e.g., optimization, innovation, transformation).
- Organizational scope. This dimension aims to detect the range or boundary of DT impact on the NPO (e.g., project-specific, organization-wide, inter-organizational).
- Organizational involvement. This dimension aims to identify the actors involved in the transformation of the NPO, or leading or enabling the DT effort (e.g., top management, grassroots teams, external partners).
- Organizational element. This dimension refers to the segment of the NPO affected by DT (e.g., service delivery, internal processes, governance).
- Operational level. This dimension aims to recognize the extent to which DT is enacted (e.g., micro/functional, meso/organizational, macro/ecosystemic).

By developing this process, the researcher classified the analyzed documents, where each article was assigned a single value per dimension, following a compatibility check that ensured coherence and prevented overlapping classifications. In other words, this process also served to classify the documents in the final dataset, while contributing to the definition of a taxonomy framework apt to classify DT initiatives in NPOs. Based on such classification, to infer latent profiles or "archetypes" within the academic discourse, the dimensions were treated as qualitative categorical variables, and the respective values as categories of such variables, forming the basis for the multivariate analysis that follows.

A Taxonomy of the Debate on DT in NPOs

As a result of the coding protocol outlined above, a total of 124 peer-reviewed journal articles were analyzed using a structured taxonomy comprising five overarching dimensions: *Digital Scope*, *Organizational Scope*, *Organizational Involvement*, *Organizational Element*, and *Operational Level*. A set of mutually exclusive values characterizes each dimension, and each article was coded into one "category" per dimension. Table 3.2 summarizes the taxonomy structure and frequency distribution across the whole corpus.

This classification shows a strong prevalence of certain technologies and scopes, such as platforms and whole-organization interventions, alongside a concentration in digitally enabled knowledge sharing and interaction beyond the routines of NPOs. At the same time, further categories of such dimensions like analytics and mobile remain comparatively underrepresented, pointing to uneven maturity across DT initiatives and related approaches/scopes to digitalization processes of NPOs.

Table 3.2 Taxonomy of the 124 articles and related frequency of the values for each dimension (adapted from Cipriano & Za, 2025)

Dimension	Category (Code)	Frequency
Digital Scope	Platform (Platform)	75
	Social Media (SocMed)	17
	Analytics (Analytics)	5
	Digital Devices (DigDevice)	13
	Software Application (SoftApp)	5
	Mobile (Mob)	9
Organizational Scope	Organizational Development (OrgDev)	22
	Knowledge Management (KnowMgt)	17
	Knowledge Sharing (KnowShar)	17
	Crowdsourcing (CrowSour)	7
	Crowdfunding (CrowFund)	6
	Social Value Creation (SocValCreat)	16
	Community Development (CommDev)	16
	Education (Edu)	15
	Co-production (CoProd)	8
Organizational Involvement	Non-profit Organization-centred (NPcentred)	70
	Public Administration & Non-profit Organization → B2C (PA&NPtoB2C)	24
	Business & Non-profit Organization ←→ Public Administration & Non-profit Organization (B&NPvsPA&NP)	13
	Hybrid Organization (HybridOrg)	3
	Non-profit Organization → Partnership (NP2Partner)	12
	Public Administration to Non-profit Organization (PA2NP)	2
Organizational Element	Digital Interaction (DigInter)	38
	Digital Process (DigProc)	30
	Digital Resource (DigRes)	35
	Digital Organizational Change (DigOrgChange)	21
Organizational Level	Whole Business (WholeBus)	84
	Amongst Inter-organizational business (InterOrg)	31
	Business Unit (BusUnit)	9
	Individual (Ind)	6

3.4 Multivariate Analysis: MCA and Clustering

Following the development of the taxonomy, this section presents the quantitative analytical phase of the study. The aim is to move beyond a dimensional classification of individual articles and toward the identification of underlying patterns, or discursive archetypes, that characterize the literature on DT in NPOs. To do so, a two-stage multivariate analysis is applied, consisting of the computation of two complementary techniques (Cipriano & Za, 2025). The *Multiple Correspondence Analysis (MCA)* is used to reduce the complexity of the categorical data derived from the taxonomy (Le Roux & Rouanet, 2004, 2009), and the *Hierarchical Clustering on Principal Components (HCPC)* is employed to group articles based on their shared taxonomic profiles (François Husson et al., 2010; Le Dien & Pagès, 2003; Ward, 1963).

This approach enables the synthesis of a fragmented and multidimensional literature by revealing clusters of studies that share common orientations in terms of DT scope, execution, or organizational focus and objectives. As such, it complements the qualitative interpretation proposed with the taxonomy by offering a data-driven lens on how DT is conceptualized and enacted in the NPO context. In particular, the taxonomy produced consists of a set of values describing the five dimensions, here assumed as categorical variables, where each article is coded according to these five mutually exclusive dimensions. To explore the relationships among these variables and the structure of the coded dataset, MCA is particularly suited. It allows for *(i) dimensionality reduction* by projecting high-dimensional categorical data into a smaller number of synthetic components that preserve the maximum amount of variance (inertia); *(ii) visualization of relationships* between categories, as well as between articles and categories; and *(iii) preparation of the data for clustering* by transforming qualitative profiles into a continuous, interpretable space (Greenacre & Blasius, 2007; Franois Husson & Josse, 2018; Johs, 2018; Le Roux & Rouanet, 2004, 2009).

Moreover, MCA does not assume linearity or normality, making it ideal for analyzing qualitative classification schemes such as taxonomies. Once MCA is performed, the HCPC technique is applied, performing as a clustering algorithm based on the reduced dimensions obtained from the MCA. That is, the HCPC allows for *(i) group articles* based on proximity in the factor space; *(ii) construct a hierarchical tree* to examine the nested structure of the data; and finally *(iii) interpret the resulting clusters* based on the frequency and prominence of specific taxonomic categories (François Husson et al., 2010; Jafarzadegan et al., 2019; Ward, 1963). Overall, this methodological combination reflects a growing trend, where qualitative data are structured and explored using exploratory multivariate techniques (Greenacre & Blasius, 2007; François Husson et al., 2010; Jorg & Michael, 1998).

The analysis was conducted using the R environment, leveraging the FactoMineR and factoextra packages (Francois Husson et al., 2020; Josse & Husson, 2016; Kostov et al., 2013), which are widely used for MCA and HCPC in social science research (François Husson et al., 2017). Starting from the taxonomy of the articles performed in the previous step, an input dataset, in the form of a binary indicator matrix (also known as a disjunctive table), was first derived to perform the MCA. In such an indicator matrix each row represents 1 of the 124 articles in the final data set, each column represents 1 of the 29 total values (as a categorical variable) across the five taxonomy dimensions, and each cell takes a value of "1" if the article was coded with a specific categorical variable and "0" otherwise. As a result, this matrix captures the whole combinatorial space of the taxonomy. Since each article is assigned only one value per dimension, each row contains exactly five "1" entries (among the 29 columns representing the categorical variables). Then, the MCA was conducted on this matrix to compute a factorial space where each axis (principal component) represents a dimension of variation in the data. First, the MCA was executed by calculation of eigenvalues, variances, and the coordinates of articles and categories in the reduced factor space (based on the indicator matrix). Second, a selection of the components was performed to maximize variability. In the present study, the first 10 principal components were retained, accounting for approximately 70% of the total inertia (i.e., variability), as they captured the most meaningful variance. Finally, clustering was performed using the computed principal components as input for the HCPC technique. This approach first applied Ward's hierarchical clustering method to build a dendrogram, which was then used to determine an optimal partitioning of the articles into distinct groups (clusters) (Ward, 1963).

To assess the robustness of the clustering solution, the following checks were applied. First, the inertia gain analysis was performed by evaluating the increase in explained variance when moving from fewer to more clusters. Afterward, the interpretability check was executed for qualitative validation of cluster composition based on the dominant category configurations. Lastly, a statistical test was run, choosing the chi-square and hypergeometric distribution tests to validate the overrepresentation of specific categories within each cluster.

As a result, the MCA yielded an interpretable factorial map that revealed the distribution of articles and taxonomy categories in a latent semantic space. Clusters were then overlaid onto this map, each representing a coherent discursive orientation toward the discussion on DT in NPOs. Accordingly, these clusters are supposed to serve multiple purposes. They act as analytical bridges between the detailed taxonomy and the more strategic conceptualization discussed in Chap. 4. They support the comparison of "families" of studies, rather than individual contributions, facilitating pattern recognition. Furthermore, they enable the theoretical generalization of the discourse, which will be used to derive problematization assumptions, strategic archetypes, and a comprehensive research agenda.

The following section presents the results of this cluster analysis in detail, including a visual map of the clusters, statistical validation, and interpretive labeling of each group.

A Cluster Analysis of the Debate on DT in NPOs

Drawing on the taxonomy developed in the previous section, the outcome of the MCA, followed by the computing of the HCPC technique, is a set of nine distinct clusters, each representing a coherent theme or strategic orientation in the DT discourse within NPOs.

The clusters are plotted using the first two principal dimensions extracted from the MCA (please note this does not refer directly to the five dimensions of the taxonomy), providing a visual mapping of articles grouped by similarity. Articles located near the barycenter of each cluster are designated as modal or "paragon" contributions, representing the most typical examples within that thematic group. Conversely, "specific" articles are situated farther from the cluster center but still reflect defining features that distinguish the cluster from others (François Husson et al., 2010, 2017; Kassambara, 2017). This approach is then helpful in describing the identity of each cluster in terms of its dominant taxonomical factors and content themes. Figure 3.1 illustrates the spatial distribution of the 124 articles plotted on the factorial plane formed by the first two dimensions (Dim 1: 10.2%, Dim 2: 9.3%) resulting from MCA.

Each point represents an individual article, and the articles are grouped into nine distinct clusters based on the results of HCPC. The convex hulls surrounding each group highlight the perimeter of the respective clusters, labeled from c.1 to c.9. These clusters reflect thematic proximity and shared characteristics based on the taxonomy dimensions analyzed. Moreover, the cluster titles were assigned based on the most representative factors and articles within each group and will serve as a foundation for the conceptual elaboration presented in Chap. 5. Hereafter, a thorough description of the nine clusters.

Cluster 1: Connecting People A strong emphasis on communication development, interaction-oriented technologies, and the use of social media defines cluster 1. Articles in this group commonly explore how nonprofit organizations use digital tools to foster engagement, dialogue, and community-building among stakeholders. The absence of more infrastructural or knowledge-management-oriented digital strategies highlights the communicative and people-centered nature of this cluster.

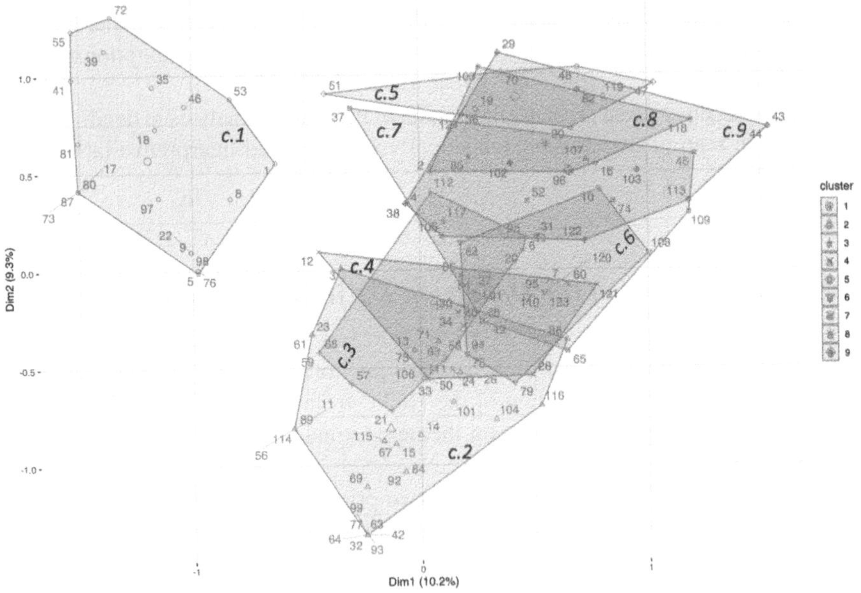

Fig. 3.1 Articles on the principal component map according to cluster (adapted from Cipriano & Za, 2025)

This thematic group emphasizes the use of digital media to amplify voices, increase inclusivity, and strengthen relational ties within communities.

Cluster 2: Innovating for Sharing Cluster 2 focuses on digital transformation efforts that enable internal innovation to promote knowledge dissemination. These contributions center on platforms, organizational development, and changes at the whole-organization level, often involving centralized digital governance. The articles typically showcase nonprofits adopting technological and strategic innovations to strengthen their ability to generate, share, and manage knowledge. Digital transformation is here portrayed as a tool for operational learning and improvement, with implications for transparency, trust-building, and institutional capacity.

Cluster 3: Creating Value This cluster groups articles that highlight digital transformation as a means of social value creation. Dominant factors include social value creation objectives, resource-intensive digital infrastructures, and intersectoral configurations involving public and nonprofit partnerships. These contributions underscore the role of technology in enabling new forms of public engagement, service delivery, and civic participation. The use of digital platforms and analytics often supports initiatives designed to increase social equity, access, and empowerment in underserved communities.

Cluster 4: Innovating for Fundraising Cluster 4 includes studies focusing on digital innovation in fundraising. Crowdfunding, digital payment tools, and campaign orchestration are central themes. These articles typically explore how nonprofit organizations mobilize resources through public and peer-to-peer support mechanisms, often involving collaborations with public institutions. Digital transformation is framed as a pathway to financial sustainability and donor engagement, with an emphasis on communication strategies, campaign design, and the affordances of digital platforms for financial support.

Cluster 5: Developing Digital Processes This cluster captures DT initiatives aimed at business process reengineering within nonprofit organizations. High-frequency factors include business unit-level transformation, analytics, and digitization of procedural workflows. Articles in this group investigate the internal dimension of digitalization, focusing on how NPOs automate and optimize administrative functions, service operations, and performance monitoring. The digital tools discussed often enable more efficient management, decision-making, and data use across various organizational levels.

Cluster 6: Innovating for Knowledge Cluster 6 addresses digital transformation aimed at improving knowledge management across organizations. The contributions highlight the development and implementation of knowledge-sharing platforms, interorganizational data exchanges, and documentation systems. These DT initiatives are typically collaborative (in nature), involving multiple actors and institutions.

Emphasis is placed on strategic knowledge creation and dissemination processes, fostering organizational memory, and enhancing decision-making capabilities.

Cluster 7: Sourcing for Digital Cluster 7 comprises articles that explore how nonprofit organizations engage in sourcing digital skills, tools, and partnerships. Dominant factors include crowdsourcing strategies and hybrid organizational forms, where nonprofits co-create or co-develop digital infrastructures with other sectors. These studies underscore the challenges and opportunities in accessing technological resources and expertise, often focusing on open-source, grassroots innovation, or capacity-building collaborations that extend beyond traditional nonprofit boundaries.

Cluster 8: Co-Producing for Innovation This cluster brings together studies emphasizing digital co-production initiatives between nonprofit organizations and public-sector actors. These collaborations aim to address complex societal issues, such as urban development, civic infrastructure, and social service innovation. Core dimensions include interorganizational collaboration, co-production logic, and large-scale digital interventions targeting public value. Technology is positioned not just as a functional tool, but as a mediating infrastructure for multistakeholder governance and inclusive service design.

Cluster 9: Innovating for Education Cluster 9 highlights the role of digital transformation in enhancing educational initiatives. Articles in this group examine how nonprofit organizations adopt digital tools to improve civic education, workforce training, and public awareness campaigns. The focus is on partnerships with educational institutions and local communities, as well as the use of mobile devices, apps, or media content to deliver learning opportunities. The strategic goal in this cluster is often empowerment through knowledge, particularly in underserved or vulnerable populations.

Each cluster thus reflects a distinct thematic pathway through which DT initiatives are discussed and operationalized within NPOs. While certain topics (e.g., communication, innovation, co-production) recur across multiple clusters, their configurations and strategic intents differ. Together, the clusters provide a rich, multidimensional portrait of how digital technologies are reshaping the structure, behavior, and societal roles of nonprofit actors. To provide a concise overview of how the analyzed articles contributed to the definition of the clusters, Fig. 3.2 displays the distribution of articles across the nine clusters identified through the applied analytical techniques.

3.5 Final Considerations

This chapter has explored the conceptual conformations and empirical structures of the debate concerning how the DT process is understood and enacted within NPOs. Through a meta-synthesis of 124 scholarly articles, a taxonomy was constructed from the literature synthesis (Nickerson et al., 2013), revealing a multidimensional

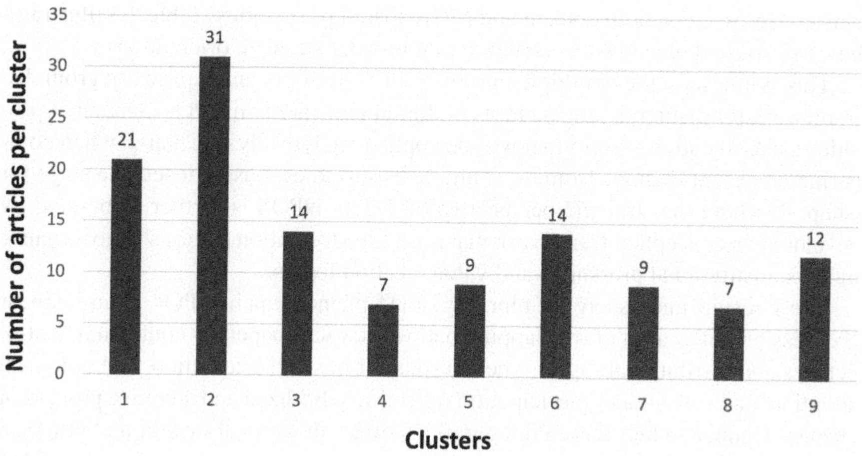

Fig. 3.2 Distribution of the 124 articles among the nine clusters

understanding of DT in NPOs, centered on five core analytical dimensions. Overall, these dimensions show the strategic orientation, technological means, collaborative structure, service or mission impact, and organizational boundary-crossing characterizing DT initiatives in NPOs. Each article in the corpus was categorized using this framework, allowing a granular and systematic representation of the diversity of DT practices and narratives. In addition, these dimensions provide the basis for classifying diverse DT initiatives along thematic lines (i.e., ranging from service delivery innovations to structural reorganizations and participatory models of change) related to *(i) what changes* (referring to the nature of the change being pursued through DT. This includes internal process optimization, external communication enhancement, service delivery reconfiguration, or hybrid goals combining multiple objectives), *(ii) how it changes* (referring to the mechanisms through which DT is enacted, such as the adoption of cloud services, platform integration, social media use, and mobile app deployment), and *who enacts it* (referring to the organizational agents and beneficiaries involved, including staff, volunteers, donors, partners, and service users).

Besides the resulting taxonomy, a subsequent cluster analysis was performed by employing the MCA and the HCPC techniques (François Husson et al., 2010; Le Roux & Rouanet, 2009). This revealed nine clusters representing distinct configurations of DT initiatives. Each cluster represented a different orientation based on the dominant combination of strategic intent, technological approach, and stakeholder engagement. For example, clusters varied from *"connecting people"* and *"co-producing for innovation"* to *"innovating for education,"* reflecting how NPOs align digital tools with mission-driven goals.

To synthesize these results and facilitate comparison with existing conceptual frameworks, a second layer of interpretation is proposed by grouping the nine clusters into four strategic archetypes. These archetypes are not abstracted de novo but rather distilled from the underlying configurations and relational patterns between clusters, drawing on both content and MCA spatial proximities. Table 3.3 illustrates how the original nine clusters coalesce into broader strategic orientations.

This synthesis serves multiple purposes. First, it offers an empirically grounded framework for distinguishing patterns of digital innovation in NPOs. Second, it provides a classification system that will be applied analytically in Chap. 6 when comparing empirical findings from the multiple case studies. Lastly, it sets the stage for Chap. 4, where the strategic perspective on DT in NPOS is further elaborated by developing a conceptual framework that links transformation patterns to governance models, institutional pressures, and value creation logics.

These results underscore the plurality of DT phenomena in NPOs, not as a linear progression but as a set of overlapping pathways, each shaped by contextual contingencies and institutional logics. The interplay of mission orientation, technological adoption, and stakeholder participation reflects a hybridized and adaptive process of change. Understanding these configurations offers theoretical insight and practical relevance for both researchers and practitioners navigating the complexities of DT processes in purpose-driven settings.

However, this study is not without limitations. First, the analysis is constrained by the scope of the reviewed literature, which, despite systematic selection, may omit gray literature, non-English publications, or more recent developments not yet captured in scholarly outputs. Second, although the taxonomy and cluster analysis reveal robust patterns, the interpretation of clusters remains partly dependent on subjective thematic coding and the granularity of article-level metadata. Third, the method captures discursive configurations rather than actual organizational outcomes, which may differ from how DT initiatives are reported in academic research.

Future research could expand on these findings by conducting longitudinal or cross-national comparisons, exploring whether and how these archetypes evolve or differ by region and policy context. Moreover, integrating primary data from nonprofit practitioners, through interviews or surveys, could provide a more grounded perspective on the mechanisms and frictions of the phenomena in practice. Finally, a promising avenue lies in examining how hybrid governance models and ecosystem-based collaboration shape the success or failure of such initiatives across the different forms or legal frameworks of the entities belonging to this sector.

Taken together, this chapter contributes to a more differentiated understanding of DT in NPOs. It lays empirical and conceptual groundwork for the theoretical

Table 3.3 Cluster archetypes and corresponding cluster configurations

Strategic archetype	Constituent clusters	Key features
Operational optimizers	Cluster 2, cluster 5	Focus on internal digital reorganization, analytics, and process digitization
Externally mobilized responders	Cluster 4, cluster 7	Triggered by funding, civic engagement, or resource sourcing needs
Participatory innovators	Cluster 1, cluster 6, cluster 8	Emphasis on user involvement, co-production, and knowledge sharing
Strategic transformers	Cluster 3, cluster 9	Organization-wide, mission-aligned, education- and value-driven transformation

modeling in Chap. 4 and the empirical validation through case studies in Chap. 5. By articulating patterns, tensions, and orientations of DT, this work seeks to inform both scholarly debate and managerial practice, offering pathways for more context-sensitive and strategically aligned transformation efforts in purpose-driven organizations.

References

Baas, J., Schotten, M., Plume, A., Côté, G., & Karimi, R. (2020). Scopus as a curated, high-quality bibliometric data source for academic research in quantitative science studies. *Quantitative Science Studies, 1*(1), 377–386. https://doi.org/10.1162/qss_a_00019

Bharadwaj, A., El Sawy, O. A., Pavlou, P. A., & Venkatraman, N. (2013). Digital business strategy: Toward a next generation of insights. *MIS Quarterly, 37*(2), 471–482. https://doi.org/10.25300/misq/2013/37:2.3

Cipriano, M., & Za, S. (2024). Non-profit organisations in the digital age: A research agenda for supporting the development of a digital transformation strategy. *Journal of Information Technology, 39*(4), 732–755. https://doi.org/10.1177/02683962231219515

Cipriano, M., & Za, S. (2025). Digital transformation of non-profit organizations: A research agenda. *Communications of the Association for Information Systems, 56*, 1118–1190. https://doi.org/10.17705/1CAIS.05643

Greenacre, M., & Blasius, J. (2007). *Multiple correspondence analysis and related methods. Statistics in the social and behavioral sciences series* (Vol. 72). Chapman & Hall/CRC. https://doi.org/10.1007/s11336-006-1579-x

Hoon, C. (2013). Meta-synthesis of qualitative case studies: An approach to theory building. *Organizational Research Methods, 16*(4), 522–556. https://doi.org/10.1177/1094428113484969

Husson, F., Josse, J., Le, S., & Mazet, J. (2020). *Package 'FactoMineR'*.

Husson, F., Josse, J., & Pagès, J. (2010). Principal component methods – hierarchical clustering – partitional clustering: Why would we need to choose for visualizing data. *Applied Mathematics Department, 17*(September).

Husson, F., Lê, S., & Pagès, J. (2017). Exploratory multivariate analysis by example using R. *International Statistical Review, 79*. https://doi.org/10.1111/j.1751-5823.2011.00159_19.x

Husson, F., & Josse, J. (2018). Multiple correspondence analysis. In *Multiple correspondence analysis for the social sciences* (pp. 31–55). Routledge.

Jafarzadegan, M., Safi-Esfahani, F., & Beheshti, Z. (2019). Combining hierarchical clustering approaches using the PCA method. *Expert Systems with Applications, 137*, 1–10. https://doi.org/10.1016/j.eswa.2019.06.064

Johs, H. (2018). *Multiple correspondence analysis for the social sciences*. Routledge Taylor & Francis Group. https://doi.org/10.4324/9781315516257

Jorg, B., & Michael, G. (1998). *Visualization of categorical data*. Elsevier. https://doi.org/10.1016/B978-0-12-299045-8.X5000-1

Josse, J., & Husson, F. (2016). missMDA: A package for handling missing values in multivariate data analysis. *Journal of Statistical Software, 70*(1). https://doi.org/10.18637/jss.v070.i01

Kassambara, A. (2017). *Practical guide to principal component methods in R*. (Stdh.com, Ed.) *Multivariate analysis II* (1st ed.).

Knote, R., Janson, A., Söllner, M., & Leimeister, J. M. (2021). Value co-creation in smart services: A functional affordances perspective on smart personal assistants. *Journal of the Association for Information System, 22*(2), 418–458. https://doi.org/10.17705/1jais.00667

Kostov, B., Bécue-Bertaut, M., & Husson, F. (2013). Multiple factor analysis for contingency tables in the FactoMineR packasge. *The R Journal, 5*(1), 29. https://doi.org/10.32614/RJ-2013-003

Kundisch, D., Muntermann, J., Oberländer, A. M., Rau, D., Röglinger, M., Schoormann, T., & Szopinski, D. (2021). An update for taxonomy designers. *Business & Information Systems Engineering*. https://doi.org/10.1007/s12599-021-00723-x

Kutzner, K., Thorsten, S., & Knackstedt, R. (2018). Digital transformation in information systems research: A taxonomy-based approach to structure the field. In *26th European Conference on Information Systems (ECIS)*.

Le Dien, S., & Pagès, J. (2003). Hierarchical multiple factor analysis: Application to the comparison of sensory profiles. *Food Quality and Preference, 14*(5–6), 397–403. https://doi.org/10.1016/S0950-3293(03)00027-2

Le Roux, B., & Rouanet, H. (2004). *Geometric data analysis from correspondence analysis to structured data analysis*. Kluwer Academic Publishers. http://www.springeronline.com

Le Roux, B., & Rouanet, H. (2009). *Multiple correspondence analysis. Quantitative applications in the social sciences*. SAGE Publications. https://doi.org/10.1177/007542429602400208

McKelvey, B. (1982). *Organizational systematics: Taxonomy, evolution, classification*. University of California Press.

Nickerson, R. C., Varshney, U., & Muntermann, J. (2013). A method for taxonomy development and its application in information systems. *European Journal of Information Systems, 22*(3), 336–359. https://doi.org/10.1057/ejis.2012.26

Pranckutė, R. (2021). Web of Science (WoS) and scopus: The titans of bibliographic information in today's academic world. *Publications 2021, 9*(1), 12. https://doi.org/10.3390/PUBLICATIONS9010012

Remane, G., Nickerson, R. C., Hanelt, A., Tesch, J. F., & Kolbe, L. M. (2016). A taxonomy of carsharing business models. In *2016 International Conference on Information Systems, ICIS 2016* (pp. 1–19).

Skinner, R. J., Nelson, R. R., & Chin, W. (2022). Synthesizing qualitative evidence: A roadmap for information systems research. *Journal of the Association for Information Systems, 23*(3), 639–677. https://doi.org/10.17705/1jais.00741

Venkatesh, V., Brown, S. A., & Bala, H. (2013). Bridging the qualitative-quantitative divide: Guidelines for conducting mixed methods research in Information systems. *MIS Quarterly, 37*(1), 21–54. https://www.jstor.org/stable/43825936

Vial, G. (2019). Understanding digital transformation: A review and a research agenda. *The Journal of Strategic Information Systems, 28*(2), 118–144. https://doi.org/10.1016/j.jsis.2019.01.003

Ward, J. H. (1963). Hierarchical grouping to optimize an objective function. *Journal of the American Statistical Association, 58*(301), 236. https://doi.org/10.2307/2282967

Chapter 4
A Strategic Framework

4.1 Conceptual Background

Drawing on the insights developed in Chaps. 2 and 3, it becomes evident that DT phenomena of NPOs constitute a distinctive and multidimensional challenge for academics and practitioners. Unlike private enterprises that often pursue digitalization with clear profit aims and defined market incentives, NPOs operate within complex ecosystems shaped by mission-driven goals, constrained resources, and heterogeneous stakeholder demands. As a result, their paths toward digitalization are rarely linear or capability-led; they are instead adaptive, contingent, and frequently fragmented.

Building on the quantitative and qualitative overview of the literature, this chapter aims to deepen the understanding of DT initiatives in NPOs by introducing a theoretically grounded and strategically oriented framework. The proposed framework draws on both empirical insights and conceptual synthesis, aiming to inform scholarly debate and managerial practice by better aligning DT approaches with the structural and normative realities of the nonprofit sector.

Whereas Chap. 3 delineated the empirical conformations of DT through a synthesis of the literature and the identification of nine archetypal configurations, this chapter transitions toward theory-building. It assumes that DT processes exceed the idea of merely technological adjustment or managerial trend, but rather trigger strategic reconfigurations shaped by a set of organizational, social, and technological dynamics. It aims to address key gaps in the literature, particularly the limited applicability of maturity models and corporate strategy frameworks to NPO contexts, by offering a lens of analysis that accounts for purpose orientation and contextual variability.

A central argument advanced in this chapter is that DT initiatives in NPOs must be approached as a sociotechnical phenomenon in which organizational intent, digital mechanisms, and institutional contexts are deeply intertwined, and not simply as

M. Cipriano, *Digital Transformation in Non-profit Organizations*, SpringerBriefs in Information Systems,
https://doi.org/10.1007/978-3-032-20937-5_4

a matter of capacity-building or operational enhancement (Cipriano & Za, 2024). This perspective aligns with established work in information systems (IS) and organization studies that emphasizes path dependency (Wessel et al., 2021), configurational strategy (Hinings et al., 2018), and strategic bricolage in response to external shocks or constraints (Cipriano & Za, 2024).

Additionally, this chapter introduces the concept of strategic dynamics to describe the drivers and feedback loops that shape how DT processes emerge and evolve within NPOs. These dynamics may be externally stimulated by policy, funding priorities, or technological advances, or internally generated, through leadership initiative, culture, or organizational learning. Understanding DT in NPOs thus requires recognizing how structural configurations and dynamic drivers interact over time.

The remainder of this chapter unfolds as follows. The next section provides a theoretical grounding for the strategic framing of DT in NPOs, highlighting tensions between instrumental and normative logics and the limits of traditional strategy frameworks. Then, the following section introduces the core framework proposed in this monograph, structured around the empirical taxonomy and enriched by the dynamic relationships captured in the visual and conceptual design. A further section represents an attempt to benchmark the proposed framework against a leading framework emerging from the literature (Matt et al., 2015), offering both comparison and contrast. The last two sections echo on the strategic implications of adopting such a perspective for nonprofit leaders and policymakers and set the stage for the empirical investigation that follows, explaining how the framework supports the analytical design of the case study presented in Chap. 5.

4.2 Theoretical Considerations: DT and Strategy

Addressing DT initiatives in NPOs requires a strategic understanding that moves beyond technology adoption to engage with institutional logics, value creation, and contextual complexity. In business-oriented literature, DT is often framed through lenses of customer-centric innovation, competitive positioning, or capability-based growth (Bharadwaj et al., 2013; Vial, 2019). However, such assumptions do not translate tidily into the nonprofit domain, where strategic success is not measured solely through performance indicators but also through legitimacy, inclusion, and mission fulfillment (George et al., 2016; Mair et al., 2015).

Mainstream DT models frequently conceptualize transformation as a maturity process, progressing through stages of awareness, experimentation, integration, and optimization (Matt et al., 2015). These models assume internal coherence, strategic foresight, and resource control, conditions that are often deficient or volatile in NPOs. As Cipriano and Za (2024) argue, many third-sector organizations instead pursue DT through configurational or path-dependent trajectories, shaped by piecemeal adoption, bricolage, and strategic adaptation in response to external pressures.

Indeed, digital initiatives in NPOs are often triggered by contingent stimuli, new policy demands, donor expectations, social needs, or crises (such as the increasing demands generated by the need to manage and obviate the challenges triggered by the COVID-19 pandemic), and develop incrementally across time and function. Rather than executing centrally coordinated strategies, organizations rely on distributed agency, improvisation, and co-production with stakeholders (Brink et al., 2020). This leads to highly variable digital configurations that are more relational than sequential, more emergent than designed.

From this perspective, it seems that strategy in NPOs cannot be conceived as an a priori plan aligned with long-term digital goals, at first. Instead, it is a socially embedded and interpretive process, shaped by internal governance structures, cultural expectations, and the dynamics of legitimacy-seeking across the ecosystem (do Adro et al., 2021; Kraus et al., 2022; Saidoun, 2025). The dual tension between internal coherence and external responsiveness, and between instrumental and normative goals, complicates strategic decision-making in ways that are (apparently) different or not accounted for by business-centric DT models.

In particular, as emerged by the thorough analysis of the literature strictly concerning the DT debate in NPOs, it seems that nonprofit-oriented digital strategy therefore operates through portfolios of initiatives, such as Customer Relationship Management (CRM) systems adoption, digital fundraising platforms, or data-driven service design, that reflect distinct logics, actors, and outcomes. These initiatives may not align with a singular strategic vision but instead form a mixture of responses to opportunities and constraints. Most importantly, they are often shaped by stakeholder participation, regulatory context, and resource volatility rather than internal capability progression (do Adro et al., 2021; Jong & Ganzaroli, 2023; Thrassou et al., 2024).

Given this complexity, it is then likely there is a need for alternative frameworks that integrate digital and organizational dimensions while accounting for mission-orientation, stakeholder multiplicity, and nonlinear strategic patterns. Such frameworks must recognize that DT in NPOs involves strategic dynamics, bidirectional relationships between organizational purpose, digital tools, operational settings, and stakeholder involvement that continuously reshape configurations over time (considering the peculiarities of the sector anyway). The framework presented in the following section addresses this need, offering a lens of analysis grounded in empirical findings and oriented toward the strategic realities of the nonprofit sector.

4.3 A Strategic Framework for Addressing DT in NPOs

This section introduces a strategic framework for designing, examining, or addressing DT initiatives in NPOs. It builds straightforwardly on the taxonomy and empirical clustering presented in Chap. 3, while advancing a visual and conceptual tool that captures the nonlinear, sociotechnical, and purpose-oriented nature of transformation processes in the sector.

In contrast to linear maturity models or business-centric transformation blueprints, this framework provides a multi-dimensional and recursive structure. It reflects how NPOs engage with digital technologies not only to optimize processes but to reconfigure their operational, governance, and relational architectures in alignment with evolving missions and ecosystems.

The rationale for presenting this framework at this stage of the monograph lies in the need to synthesize the empirical diversity observed in Chap. 2 into a coherent strategic logic. The literature clusters and archetypes derived from the taxonomy showed that NPOs adopt divergent pathways of digital engagement, shaped by contextual contingencies, institutional missions, and resource constraints. Any theoretical model aiming for strategic relevance must therefore embrace this diversity, while providing interpretive clarity.

The proposed model incorporates two cross-cutting logics already latent in the taxonomy. First, it emphasizes the *Stimulus vs. Effect* purpose inspired by how DT initiatives emerge and materialize. Second, it draws on two overarching perspectives being adopted in the examination of the DT phenomenon, and central to some mainstream research characterizing the IS discipline, that is, the *Organizational vs. Technological* perspective, reflecting the sociotechnical integration.

Then, according to the dimensions emerged from the taxonomy of the literature (as presented in Chap. 3), these dimensions are positioned into the intersecting axes of the two logics above, structuring the framework into four external quadrants, with a fifth central node, represented by the *Organizational Involvement* dimension, serving as a nexus and enabler of transformation (in this specific context, and aligning with the nonprofit domain). In this way, the framework offers not a prescriptive roadmap, but a flexible tool to interpret how DT phenomena unfold, adapt, and reflect deeper institutional dynamics.

Specifically, the five components of the framework draw directly from the dimensions of the taxonomy, where the *Digital Scope* dimension aims to capture the range, type, and role of digital tools, platforms, and infrastructures involved in the transformation initiative. It reflects technological breadth and ambition, ranging from back-office automation to data platforms and participatory apps. The *Organizational Scope* dimension denotes the areas of organizational value creation targeted by DT, such as fundraising, service delivery, advocacy, or knowledge sharing. It reflects how digital intent intersects with mission delivery. The *Organizational Element* dimension refers to the internal structures, processes, and rules affected by digital interventions. It includes governance configurations, workflows, and decision-making practices impacted by digital change. The *Operational Level* dimension identifies the scale and organizational locus of transformation, from department-level adjustments to whole-system reconfigurations. It also captures whether DT efforts are centralized, decentralized, or networked. Finally, the *Organizational Involvement* dimension, positioned at the center of the framework, represents the group of actors, staff, leadership, volunteers, and stakeholders, actively engaged in, or impacted by, the DT initiative. This central role reflects both the relational complexity and participatory dynamics observed in NPO transformations. Rather than treating involvement as a passive condition, the framework conceptualizes it as a strategic driver, where DT is translated into practice, co-created, and contested.

Still, a key feature of the framework is its explicit representation of sociotechnical coupling. It aims to distinguish three different types of characters that could act either as drivers or inhibitors for DT initiatives in NPOs. First, it assumes the presence of *Strategic Stimuli* (e.g., the double-oriented solid arrows; for this purpose, it is considered the outward direction from the central node). These stimuli represent proactive forces initiated by organizational actors, such as leadership vision, mission-aligned experimentation, or stakeholder-driven demands, that radiate toward the external quadrants to shape technological or organizational developments.

Second, it assumes the presence of *Feedback Dynamics* given the strategic stimuli (for this purpose, it is considered the returning direction, from the quadrants to the center). These dynamics represent reconfiguration loops, where the effects of digital implementation in one area (e.g., changes in governance or user engagement) affect others simultaneously or reshape them over time (e.g., organizational sensemaking, norms, or strategic direction).

Third, it assumes the possibility of *Cross-Quadrant Influence* among the dimensions. The diagram also captures bidirectional feedback loops between opposite quadrants (e.g., *Organizational Scope* ↔ *Operational Level*, *Digital Scope* ↔ *Organizational Element*, depicted as double-oriented dotted arrows), representing the recursive interplay between social goals and operational routines, or between digital capabilities and structural governance. These arrows attempt to make visible the nonlinear pathways through which transformation can evolve.

Overall, the proposed layered logic reflects the theoretically derived observation that DT in NPOs rarely follows a single trajectory. Instead, it seems to emerge recursively, reacting to outcomes, stakeholder responses, and contextual pressures. Specifically, evidence of this logic comes from the DT archetypes identified in Chap. 2. For example, the cluster including discussions focused on *"co-production and platform"* exemplifies two dimensions of the taxonomy, representing high *Organizational Involvement* driving *Digital Scope* expansion. Here, it emerges that collaborative platforms were adopted not only as technical tools but as expressions of participatory governance. The resulting process redesigns (representing the *Organizational Element* dimension) in turn generated new feedback around accountability and inclusion, reshaping engagement strategies. Further reasoning concerns the cluster, including discussions related to *"back-office digitalization,"* representing targeted technological change, often initiated through external funding or compliance pressures. Here, the *Digital Scope* dimension seems to represent a stimulus, but the transformation remained bounded within internal workflows and to a certain extent in terms of *Operational Level*. This reflects a more linear but still adaptive trajectory, where strategic feedback was constrained but present. In addition, the cluster, including discussions on *"advocacy and outreach,"* appears to highlight that external social demands or legitimacy challenges trigger DT initiatives emerging from the Organizational Scope dimension. As a result, in certain circumstances, the organization's response was to develop digital communication capabilities (*Digital Scope* dimension) and open new channels of stakeholder interaction. From this perspective, it seems that the above logic on the feedback loop affected both structural routines and digital experimentation.

These examples show how unique dimensions can be engaged in different sequences, with different roles (stimulus or effect), depending on the configuration of involvement, context, and mission. Figure 4.1 depicts the proposed framework aiming to interpret these differences without forcing convergence.

To summarize, the strategic framework proposed here (afterward recalled with the label *"NPOs DT framework"*) advances from prescriptive models of transformation to embrace a situated, recursive, and purpose-driven view of DT in NPOs. By centering the *Organizational Involvement* dimension and mapping the dynamics of both proactive influence and strategic reconfiguration, the framework respects the pluralism and contextuality inherent in the third sector. It aims to offer researchers a conceptual lens for analyzing DT trajectories without imposing linear assumptions and provides practitioners with a reflective tool to assess where DT is emerging, why, and how it might evolve in light of internal agency and ecosystem demands.

In the next section, this model is contrasted with an influential DT framework from the corporate literature (Matt et al., 2015), to further underscore its distinctive contribution to the study and practice of digital transformation in mission-oriented, stakeholder-driven organizations.

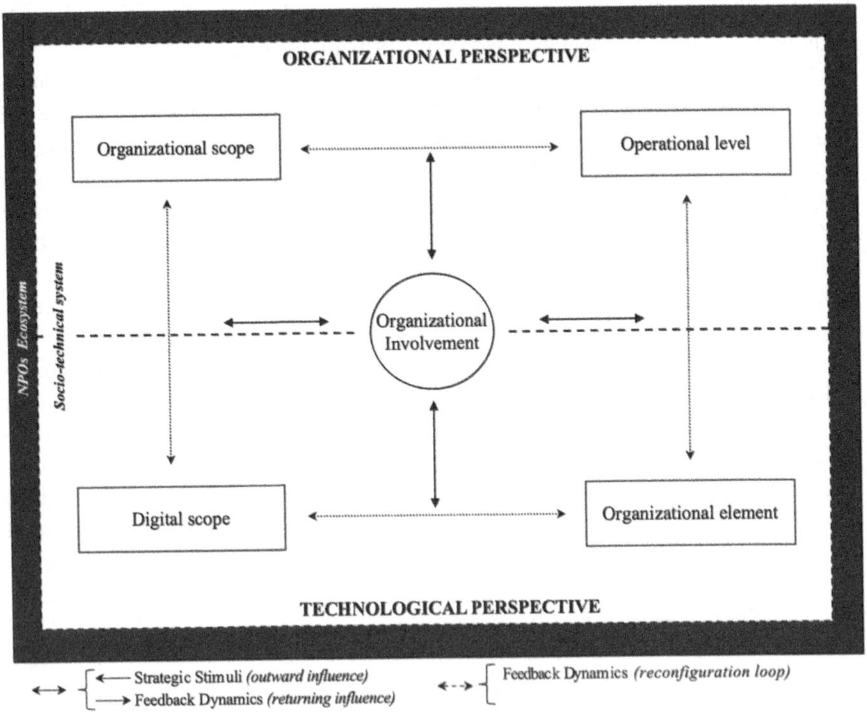

Fig. 4.1 A strategic framework for addressing DT in NPOs (adapted from Cipriano & Za, 2024)

4.4 Benchmarking with For-Profit DT Frameworks: A Comparative Lens

To better contextualize the strategic framework introduced in Fig. 4.1, this section benchmarks it against established corporate-oriented models of DT, focusing in particular on one of the first influential DT frameworks, appearing in the literature (Matt et al., 2015). Among others, this study refers to the DT framework proposed by Matt et al. (2015), which consists of four core dimensions (i.e., the *Use of Technologies*, *Changes in Value Creation*, *Structural Changes*, and *Financial Aspects)*, that collectively describe how organizations conceptualize and implement digital change. The *Use of Technologies* dimension reflects a company's strategic orientation toward digital tools and platforms, encompassing both its openness to adopting new technologies and its ambition to leverage IT for competitive advantage. *Changes in Value Creation* pertain to the ways DT reshapes how value is generated and delivered, including its effects on product and service innovation, customer interaction, and the competencies required to support evolving business models. The *Structural Changes* dimension addresses the internal organizational modifications necessitated by digital initiatives, ranging from incremental adjustments in processes to the creation of new roles, departments, or business units when transformation becomes central to the firm's strategy. Lastly, the *Financial Aspects* dimension concerns the economic rationale and investment logic of DT, including how resources are allocated, expected returns are calculated, and digital initiatives are prioritized within broader financial planning. Together, these four dimensions provide a comprehensive view of how DT is strategized and operationalized within corporate settings. In particular, these four dimensions are claimed to be governed by a layer of Strategic Leadership. In this study, given its peculiarities, this proposition is conceived as one designed for-profit-oriented objectives (e.g., for commercial enterprises). Accordingly, the Matt et al. (2015) framework is here taken as a useful basis for comparison, revealing the distinct assumptions, priorities, and structural logic that differentiate DT in NPOs.

Conceptual Divergence: Purpose, Agency, and Dynamics

At the core of the difference between the two paradigms framing the frameworks under analysis (i.e., for-profit-oriented and nonprofit-oriented ones), it seems to be the strategic intent underpinning transformation. For example, focusing on the Matt et al. (2015) assumptions, the DT strategy appears to be treated as a top-down initiative, oriented toward competitiveness, efficiency, and innovation-driven growth. The role of leadership is centralized, often tied to executive roles like Chief Digital Officers (CDOs), and change is seen as orchestrated and deliberate. In contrast, NPOs operate in environments shaped by mission fulfillment, legitimacy, and multistakeholder collaboration. As evidenced in the empirical synthesis (see Chap. 3),

NPOs rarely pursue DT through a singular strategic plan. Instead, transformation emerges from a distributed ecology of actors, values, and constraints. Thus, while the Matt et al. (2015) DT framework assumes strategic coherence, the proposed framework (see Fig. 3.1) for NPOs embraces strategic pluralism and adaptive reconfiguration. This divergence becomes particularly salient when it comes to accounting for certain characteristics of DT in NPOs, especially considering the *Organizational Involvement* dimension. Positioned at the center of the proposed *NPOs DT framework*, this dimension captures the governance, co-creation, and interpretive work of DT initiatives. It acknowledges that in the nonprofit context, transformation is not simply executed, it is negotiated, legitimated, and often emergent.

Hence, in proceeding with the comparison between the two frameworks, both the purpose and suitability of each possible association between their respective dimensions have been carefully considered, with attention to identifying key commonalities and differences. First, a clear connection emerged between the *"Use of technology"* dimension (DT framework) and the *"Digital Scope"* dimension (*NPOs DT framework).* In contrast, for the other cases, two dimensions of the *NPOs DT framework* were associated with one of the DT framework (Matt et al., 2015). Specifically, the *"Changes in value creation"* dimension (DT framework) was associated with the *"Organizational Scope"* and *"Organizational Involvement"* dimensions (*NPOs DT framework),* and the *"Structural changes"* dimension (DT framework) was associated with the *"Organizational Change"* and *"Organizational Operation"* dimensions (*NPOs DT framework).* The comparative results of this analysis are presented in Table 4.1, which summarizes the structural mapping between the two frameworks, integrating both alignment and conceptual additions.

Concerning the *Use of Technologies* dimension, the identification of an NPO's level of ambition toward a specific technology (*Digital Scope* dimension) can be understood as a determinant of its strategic orientation and the internal capabilities required for implementation. A further point of alignment can be found in the connection between *Changes in Value Creation* and the dimensions of *Organizational Scope* and *Organizational Involvement.* In this case, the extent to which an NPO intends to modify or extend its core mission through digital initiatives influences the way digital activities affect its value generation processes. The *Organizational Scope* dimension reflects whether digitalization is intended to enhance existing operations or to enable the pursuit of new avenues. Moreover, consistent with the empirical findings, various external actors may contribute to changes in how value is created within NPOs. Such interactions can lead to significant modifications in the organization's business model. The final correspondence relates to *Structural Changes*, which can be associated with *Organizational Element* and *Operational Level.* The identification of the expected structural modifications resulting from DT helps clarify which components of the organization will be impacted and how such changes will be positioned. While *Organizational Element* refers to the integration of digital technologies into the existing organizational setup, *Operational Level* addresses the specific levels or units responsible for implementing these initiatives.

Table 4.1 Comparison between for-profit and nonprofit-oriented DT frameworks

DT framework dimensions	NPOs DT framework dimensions	Interpretive notes
Use of Technologies (Matt et al., 2015)	Digital Scope	Both frameworks address technological ambition; in NPOs, tools are aligned with mission fulfillment rather than market advantage.
Changes in Value Creation (Matt et al., 2015)	Organizational Scope + Organizational Involvement	NPO value creation is socially, not economically, defined. Involvement reflects how external actors shape and are shaped by DT processes.
Structural Changes (Matt et al., 2015)	Organizational Element + Operational Level	The proposed framework for NPOs adds granularity by separating internal structures (Element) from scale and locus (Level).
Financial Aspects (Matt et al., 2015)	(No equivalent)	So far, the analysis concerning DT initiatives in NPOs has not revealed a direct conversation concerning how the financial aspect shapes the DT process in NPOs. Financial constraints exist but are often externalized (e.g., grants, funding rules). These were not analytically prominent in our dataset.
Strategic character		
Strategic Leadership (layer) (Matt et al., 2015)	Organizational Involvement (core mediator)	The proposed framework for NPOS decentralizes leadership, foregrounding distributed agency, legitimacy--building, and stakeholder coordination.

This, in turn, informs the type of knowledge or competencies that may need to be developed or acquired.

In summary, the proposed strategic framework for addressing DT in NPOs (see Fig. 4.1) captures not only the commonly addressed dimensions found in broader DT literature but also introduces tailored dimensions specifically suited to the analysis of DT initiatives within NPOs. Notably, financial aspects (although emerging from theoretical groundwork) were intentionally excluded, as these were not substantiated by the evidence examined in the present analyses. Furthermore, while a clear correspondence can be observed between the *Use of Technologies* and *Digital Scope* dimensions, the *NPOs DT framework* enables a more nuanced exploration of DT in NPOs. This is made possible through the association of two distinct dimensions within the taxonomy (see Chap. 3) to a single dimension in the Matt et al. (2015) framework in two instances, thereby offering a more granular perspective on transformation processes in nonprofit mission-driven contexts.

The Organizational Involvement as Strategic Enabler

A key conceptual contribution introduced by the proposed *NPOs DT framework* lies in the explicit recognition of *Organizational Involvement* as a strategic enabler. Unlike the approach adopted by Matt et al. (2015), in which strategy is conceived as a top-down managerial layer that governs transformation from above, *Organizational Involvement* is instead understood as the arena in which transformation is shaped, contested, and realized through bottom-up dynamics. This perspective does not negate the role of leadership but redefines it as distributed, networked, and contingent upon the specific governance structures and mission-oriented ethos of NPOs. This reinterpretation is especially pertinent in mission-oriented/purpose-driven organizations, where legitimacy is co-constructed and strategic direction frequently emerges through participatory processes (e.g., bottom-up experimentation), alignment with external actors, or normative discourse. In other words, DT initiatives must be viewed as morally appropriate, mission-aligned, and socially justified by those both within and outside NPOs. Accordingly, *Organizational Involvement* dimension serves both as a generator of strategic stimuli and as a receiver of feedback effects, underscoring its dual role as both a driver and a consequence (e.g., input and outcome) of transformation dynamics.

4.5 Final Considerations

Drawing on the comparative analysis between corporate DT approaches and the dynamics observed within nonprofit contexts, several cross-cutting implications can be identified. First, DT in NPOs tends to be purpose-led rather than performance-driven. This distinction shapes not only the direction and content of transformation but also who defines it and how outcomes are evaluated. Second, the framework developed in this study allows for configurational flexibility, supporting transformation processes that emerge from different stimuli (such as technological, organizational, or participatory) and evolve through recursive feedback loops rather than rigid, linear sequencing. Third, a defining feature of the proposed model is its emphasis on ecosystemic agency. Transformation is not driven by centralized leadership alone, but through the interaction of a heterogeneous network of actors (including staff, volunteers, funders, users), each influencing and interpreting the change process. Additionally, the model favors a logic of dynamic alignment over static strategic balance. Rather than aiming for equilibrium across predefined domains, the framework highlights the importance of temporal and contextual alignment, where stimuli, co-creation, and feedback continuously reshape the transformation pathway.

From a theoretical standpoint, the proposed framework extends prevailing DT literature by embedding a multidimensional and recursive understanding of change that accounts for the normative, participatory, and resource-constrained characteristics of third-sector organizations. Notably, the reconceptualization of strategic agency through the *Organizational Involvement* dimension shifts the analytical lens from centralized command to decentralized, negotiated, and context-contingent processes. In this respect, the framework integrates insights from stakeholder theory, collective sense-making, and emergent strategy logics, providing a sociotechnical account of how transformation is initiated, governed, and sustained in NPOs. Furthermore, by complementing existing models, the proposed framework offers greater granularity in understanding structural and operational reconfigurations. It places stronger emphasis on legitimacy-building, co-production, and iterative learning, thereby contributing a more nuanced and adaptable framework for studying and designing digital strategies in the nonprofit domain. The attention to stimuli and feedback also introduces a temporal logic that helps explain how digital initiatives evolve, hinge on, or scale over time.

From a practical standpoint, the proposed framework serves as a lens of analysis/diagnostic and planning tool for managers, consultants, and digital strategists working within NPOs. By clarifying five interconnected dimensions and their relationships, it facilitates identification of suitable entry points for transformation, assessment of organizational readiness, alignment of stakeholder interests, and revision of strategy in response to contextual dynamics. Its modular structure intends to allow NPOs to tailor their digital pathways according to mission, capabilities, and environmental conditions.

In terms of future research directions, major opportunities concern advancing the utility and validation of such a framework. Empirical application through longitudinal or comparative case studies would allow for testing and refinement of its components in diverse nonprofit settings. Future studies may also investigate how different dimensional configurations correlate with transformation outcomes such as digital maturity, legitimacy gains, or operational resilience. For example, drawing from the typologies identified in Chap. 2, analyses could be pursued to explore patterns of DT and organizational adaptation. Additionally, the framework may inform the design of readiness assessment tools adapted explicitly to other organizations of the third sector, as well as support practitioner-facing resources for strategy development and reflection. That is, expanding the scope of the framework to include hybrid and mission-driven organizations operating in the broader third sector could further enhance its relevance and generalizability. Ultimately, participatory co-design with practitioners could support iterative improvements and ensure contextual grounding of the model in real-world decision-making environments.

Hence, given these conceptual and practical considerations, the next chapter presents a multiple case study investigation aimed at empirically applying and testing the framework developed in this study. The objective is to explore how NPOs engage with DT across diverse contexts, and how the proposed dimensions manifest in real-world strategic processes.

References

Bharadwaj, A., El Sawy, O. A., Pavlou, P. A., & Venkatraman, N. (2013). Digital business strategy: Toward a next generation of insights. *MIS Quarterly, 37*(2), 471–482. https://doi.org/10.25300/MISQ/2013/37:2.3

Brink, H., Packmohr, S., & Vogelsang, K. (2020). Fields of action to advance the digital transformation of NPOs – Development of a framework. In *Lecture Notes in Business Information Processing* (Vol. 398, pp. 82–97). https://doi.org/10.1007/978-3-030-61140-8_6

Cipriano, M., & Za, S. (2024). Non-profit organisations in the digital age: A research agenda for supporting the development of a digital transformation strategy. *Journal of Information Technology, 39*(4), 732–755. https://doi.org/10.1177/02683962231219515

do Adro, F., Fernandes, C. I., Veiga, P. M., & Kraus, S. (2021). Social entrepreneurship orientation and performance in non-profit organizations. *International Entrepreneurship and Management Journal, 17*(4), 1591–1618. https://doi.org/10.1007/s11365-021-00748-4

George, G., Howard-Grenville, J., Joshi, A., & Tihanyi, L. (2016). Understanding and tackling societal grand challenges through management research. *Academy of Management Journal, 59*(6), 1880–1895. https://doi.org/10.5465/AMJ.2016.4007;JOURNAL:JOURNAL:AMJ;PAGEGROUP:STRING:PUBLICATION

Hinings, B., Gegenhuber, T., & Greenwood, R. (2018). Digital innovation and transformation: An institutional perspective. *Information and Organization, 28*(1), 52–61. https://doi.org/10.1016/j.infoandorg.2018.02.004

Jong, C. L. K., & Ganzaroli, A. (2023). Managing digital transformation for social good in non-profit organizations: The case of The Felix Project zeroing hunger in London. *VOLUNTAS: International Journal of Voluntary and Nonprofit Organizations*. https://doi.org/10.1007/s11266-023-00597-5

Kraus, S., Durst, S., Ferreira, J. J., Veiga, P., Kailer, N., & Weinmann, A. (2022). Digital transformation in business and management research: An overview of the current status quo. *International Journal of Information Management, 63*(August 2020), 102466. https://doi.org/10.1016/j.ijinfomgt.2021.102466

Mair, J., Mayer, J., & Lutz, E. (2015). Navigating institutional plurality: Organizational governance in hybrid organizations. *Organization Studies, 36*(6), 713–739. https://doi.org/10.1177/0170840615580007

Matt, C., Hess, T., & Benlian, A. (2015). Digital transformation strategies. *Business & Information Systems Engineering, 57*(5), 339–343. https://doi.org/10.1007/s12599-015-0401-5

Saidoun, A. (2025). Digital transformation project in a non-profit organisation: The case of a worldwide humanitarian aid association. *Open Journal of Business and Management, 13*(04), 2626–2639. https://doi.org/10.4236/ojbm.2025.134139

Thrassou, A., Vrontis, D., Efthymiou, L., & Theofanous, G. (2024). Delineating non-profit organisations: Economy, industries and context. In *Palgrave studies of cross-disciplinary business research, in association with EuroMed Academy of Business* (Vol. Part F3311, pp. 1–20). Palgrave Macmillan. https://doi.org/10.1007/978-3-031-62530-5_1

Vial, G. (2019). Understanding digital transformation: A review and a research agenda. *Journal of Strategic Information Systems, 28*(2), 118–144. https://doi.org/10.1016/j.jsis.2019.01.003

Wessel, L., Baiyere, A., Ologeanu-Taddei, R., Cha, J., & Blegind Jensen, T. (2021). Unpacking the difference between digital transformation and IT-enabled organizational transformation. *Journal of the Association for Information Systems, 22*(1), 102–129. https://doi.org/10.17705/1jais.00655

Chapter 5
Empirical Evidence: A Multiple-Case Study

5.1 Conceptual Background

Drawing on the strategic framework presented in Chap. 4 and the taxonomy and cluster analysis presented in Chap. 3, this chapter explores how DT unfolds in the lived experience of some NPOs. In comparison with the previous chapters (that offered conceptual clarity and structural modeling), this chapter draws on the findings of a qualitative empirical study aimed at advancing the understanding of DT in NPOs by exploring how such transformations advance in practice (Cipriano et al., 2023). Specifically, a multiple-case study design (Yin, 2018) is adopted to examine 10 NPOs based in the United Kingdom (UK) operating in diverse domains such as social care, education, advocacy, disability services, and environmental activism.

Accordingly, this chapter is not intended to seek generalization; instead, it aims to provide interpretive insight into the dynamics and preconditions that shape DT initiatives in mission-oriented, resource-constrained environments like NPOs. The focus is on examining how digital changes affect organizational identity, stakeholder expectations, and operational capacity. In doing so, several questions raised in earlier sections are addressed, such as *which factors catalyze or inhibit DT initiatives in NPOs? How do different actors influence DT in NPOs? What governance adjustments, tensions, or trade-offs emerge from the real world?*

From this perspective, the case study approach was chosen to capture the complex, context-sensitive nature of DT processes in such mission-oriented organizations. Each case was selected through a purposive sampling strategy to ensure variability in size, scope, and digital maturity while maintaining a common focus on organizations with clear social objectives (Cipriano et al., 2023). Hence, this design facilitates comparative insights while preserving depth and contextual integrity (Eisenhardt, 1989; Gioia et al., 2013).

The case descriptions and supporting data were obtained through in-depth interviews, secondary documentation, and publicly available organizational materials

M. Cipriano, *Digital Transformation in Non-profit Organizations*, SpringerBriefs in Information Systems,
https://doi.org/10.1007/978-3-032-20937-5_5

(including information directly gathered on the official websites of the UK Government). The case materials were thematically analyzed using a hybrid coding strategy, combining inductive theme generation with analytical categories informed by the preceding chapters (specifically, the taxonomy in Chap. 3 and the strategic framework in Chap. 4). That is, the coding draws conceptual alignment from earlier chapters, and, at the same time, particular attention was taken to avoid circular reasoning or framework imposition. Empirical patterns were first grounded in the data and subsequently interpreted in light of the broader analytical frame.

As a way of explanation, the selected case, which then deliberately agreed to participate in this research anonymously, emerged randomly from an attempt to involve approximately 40 NPOs operating in the Hampshire area in the UK. To classify the cases in a transparent and analytically sound way, each organization was coded based on three attributes: domain of activity, scope of operation, and size. The domain classification echoes the primary mission or thematic area (e.g., environmental, advocacy, health) of the NPOs. Scope of operation distinguishes whether an NPO is local, regional, or national in reach, based on what was stated in the case documentation (e.g., "*operating nationally*" or "*serving local communities*"). Size was coded using descriptions directly available in the data (e.g., "*small local charity*" or "*large national player*"). No external reinterpretation was applied; where no explicit scale was indicated, the most conservative interpretation was retained (e.g., "*small*" when organizational resources or staffing were described as limited). This classification supports a contextualized comparison across cases while preserving the integrity of the original materials. Overall, the case materials include public reports, organizational documents, and curated accounts, allowing for consistent cross-case comparison. Table 5.1 summarizes the information concerning the 10 NPOs analyzed.

The case identifiers (from NPO-A to NPO-J) will be used throughout the remainder of this chapter to preserve coherence, ensure anonymity, and facilitate traceable analysis. Hence, by grounding the analysis in empirical evidence, this chapter provides a more contextualized understanding of transformation pathways. It also lays the groundwork for synthesizing insights across all Chapters, where theoretical contributions and future research directions are elaborated (see Chap. 6).

5.2 Data Collection and Coding Strategy

The empirical data for this research were generated through 10 semi-structured interviews, one per case organization, conducted with a representative of the NPOs, showing different profiles (roles in the NPO and background). The interviews were carried out in-person or remotely (via Zoom or MS Teams) over 4 months and typically lasted between 45 and 120 min. All conversations were audio-recorded with participant consent, transcribed verbatim, and anonymized in line with ethical research protocols. Interviewees were recruited after initial contact with a broader

Table 5.1 Case classification summary (adapted from Cipriano et al., 2023)

Case ID	Size (people involved)	Scope	Domain	Interviewee
NPO-A	Medium (4 officers, 70 volunteers, university students)	Local CIC	Digital Inclusion & Community Cinema	F-49 Founder
NPO-B	Medium (7 trustees, 80 volunteers)	Local C (a.f.)	Family Support & Early Childhood	F-54 Coordinator
NPO-C	Large (1 founder, 6 board members, 2650 volunteers)	National SE	Financial Literacy & Advocacy	M-58 Founder
NPO-D	Medium (5 managers, 30 volunteers)	Local CIC	Military History Education	M-35 General manager
NPO-E	Large (14 trustees, 30 employees, 36 volunteers)	Local CLG (a.f.)	Emergency and Social Advice Services	F-61 Leader
NPO-F	Small (8 directors, 15 volunteers)	Local CIC	Film Education & Inclusion	M-67 Financial manager
NPO-G	Medium (10 trustees, collaborative engineers/educators/experts/advocates)	Regional PCLG	Urban Design & Mobility Advocacy	F-50 Head of partnership & public affairs
NPO-H	Small (9 trustees, 8 volunteers)	Local C	Art Promotion & Visual Education	F-47 director
NPO-I	Medium (5 trustees, 80 volunteers)	Local IC	Literacy Support & Education	M-30 Social media & program manager
NPO-J	Large (7 trustees, 96 employees, 62 volunteers)	Regional IC	Elderly Care & Social Services	M-33 Project manager for digital inclusion

group of approximately 40 UK-based NPOs, operating predominantly in the Hampshire region. Participation was voluntary and based on willingness and availability. The roles and profiles of those interviewed are summarized in Table 5.1. The interviews aimed to gain interpretive insight into how DT was framed, initiated, and navigated across diverse NPO contexts.

The interview protocol was developed based on the conceptual insights discussed in the previous Chapters (i.e., the taxonomy of DT in and the strategic framework for assessing DT in NPOs). These frameworks were employed to design the semi-structured interview protocol. Four core thematic areas for investigation were identified: organizational configuration, technology use and integration, work practices and operational dynamics, and change management and adaptation. Within each of these areas, two guiding questions were developed to prompt open-ended reflection and concrete examples. Hence, particular attention was paid to the way the representative described their NPO's starting points about technological readiness, cultural attitudes, leadership support, funding structures, as well as the relational context in which digital change was embedded (e.g., funding, policy shifts).

For example, in exploring organizational configuration, interviewees were asked how their NPOs were structured in terms of resources, competencies, and internal workflows, and how such configurations supported their service delivery. The second area, technology use, focused on the types of technologies deployed, the motivations for their adoption, and how they were embedded in practice. The third area explored daily routines, skill development, coordination mechanisms, and the use of digital tools in service delivery. Finally, the interviews addressed broader organizational changes, including those prompted by external shocks such as the COVID-19 pandemic, and how such disruptions were managed.

The data analysis, employing the NVivo software, was conducted adopting a grounded theory approach, following the three-stage coding methodology proposed by Corbin and Strauss (1990). In the first phase, open coding is applied to identify recurring concepts, issues, and language directly from the data. This stage produced a rich set of initial codes, which included references to digital applications, funding challenges, internal resistance, role changes, and external partnerships. These codes were data-driven and not tied to any predefined framework (thus, providing relevant insight for comparison with previously developed conceptual frameworks).

In the second phase, axial coding was applied to begin clustering the open codes into more abstract categories, focusing on relationships between them. For instance, assume codes related to "staff adaptation," "peer learning," and "retraining," those would have been grouped under a broader theme of "internal capability-building." This allowed the identification of broader dynamics such as how mission logics influenced technology decisions, or how external funders shaped digital agendas. Ultimately, selective coding was employed to refine and integrate the central themes across cases. At this stage, the emerging categories were evaluated in relation to the overarching analytical focus: understanding the preconditions, drivers, and organizational responses to DT (for the NPOs analyzed). The aim was to construct a coherent narrative that retained fidelity to the data while enabling interpretive insight.

Thus, while the coding process was informed by dimensions introduced in earlier chapters (e.g., digital scope, organizational involvement), no rigid imposition of those categories was applied. Themes emerged inductively from the data, ensuring that the analytical structure remained grounded in lived experiences of the participants. The subsequent sections present the empirical findings organized around key cross-case themes, supported by direct quotes from the interviews. These patterns show how transformation was experienced on the ground, how NPOs adapted their practices, and what tensions or enablers shaped the process across diverse contexts.

5.3 Empirical Patterns and Cross-Case Themes

The analysis of the 10 case studies revealed a series of recurring dynamics that characterize how NPOs are navigating DT in practice. Rather than following a linear or universal path, the transformation processes observed reflect a heterogeneous set of experiences, shaped by organizational mission, resource constraints, technological readiness, and external pressures. This section distills these patterns into five cross-case themes, each illuminating a different facet of the DT journey in NPOs.

These themes represent interlocking dimensions that offer a multiperspective understanding of how NPOs experience and respond to digital change and do not represent mutually exclusive categories. Each theme is supported by illustrative examples and quotes from the cases, highlighting both commonalities and contextual differences across organizational types and domains. The ambition is to provide interpretive insight into recurring configurations, tensions, and adaptive responses.

DT as a Function of Organizational Identity and Mission

One of the most salient cross-case insights concerns how NPOs interpret and frame DT initiatives in relation to their core mission and identity. Across the cases, DT was not seen as a neutral or purely technical endeavor, but as a process filtered through organizational purpose, values, and historical trajectories. For many NPOs, digital innovation was not primarily about efficiency or modernization, but rather about enabling, extending, or safeguarding their social objectives.

This perspective was especially evident in NPOs where the mission carried strong social inclusion or educational commitments, such as NPO-A and NPO-H. In these cases, it emerges that DT was framed as an enabler of mission fulfillment, particularly by enhancing accessibility, participation, or visibility. For example, the founder of NPO-A explained: *"Digital tools help us connect communities that might otherwise be left out. It is not just about being up-to-date, it is about being accessible."* In this context, DT was understood as a natural extension of the organization's inclusive ethos, with platforms such as online ticketing systems, virtual screenings, or hybrid events used to overcome physical and economic barriers. Similarly, NPO-H, which focuses on artistic engagement and education, described how digital technology allowed it to reimagine participation. The director explained: *"We want people from all walks of life to experience art. Sometimes, that means bringing exhibitions online or using digital workshops, whatever it takes to reach beyond the gallery walls."*

In contrast, other NPOs such as NPO-C and NPO-G adopted a more instrumental framing of DT. For these organizations, which operate in the fields of financial advocacy and urban design, respectively, DT was linked to strategic influence, operational visibility, and policy engagement. Rather than positioning digital tools as primarily inclusive, these NPOs viewed them as levers for systemic impact and external legitimacy. For instance, the founder of NPO-C claimed: *"We are here to campaign for a better financial system. That means being seen, being credible, and reaching people where they are, and that is digital."* This aspect shows a shift in how identity interacts with DT: rather than serving primarily internal needs or client access, in this case, digital capabilities were harnessed to amplify advocacy, craft persuasive narratives, and enhance institutional standing in broader networks.

This variation in framing reveals how organizational identity shapes the very meaning and ambition of DT. In some cases, DT was seen as a means of deepening existing practices (e.g., expanding reach, streamlining community engagement). In others, it served as a strategic catalyst for organizational repositioning, legitimacy, or external influence. Notably, some interviewees expressed concern about misalignments between digital trends and mission fidelity, particularly where pressures to "go digital" might risk undermining core values. This was most clearly articulated by the coordinator of NPO-B, a family support charity rooted in relational care: *"We are not a digital-first organisation, and we are careful about that. Our work is built on face-to-face connection, that is the heart of what we do."* Here, DT was cautiously integrated, primarily for enhancing support functions (e.g., for scheduling or volunteer coordination), but deliberately limited in areas seen as core to the identity and emotional labor of the service. This perspective highlights a values-based resistance to certain forms of transformation, challenging the assumption that DT is always beneficial or desirable.

Across the board, DT initiatives were not experienced uniformly but were interpreted through the lens of organizational purpose. Even when adopting similar technologies (e.g., cloud services, digital ticketing, virtual workshops), the motivations, expectations, and boundaries of use varied widely, depending on how "digital" aligned with the organization's self-conception, beneficiary expectations, and legitimacy claims. In short, the relationship between DT and organizational identity in NPOs appears to be not linear or uniform, but somewhat shaped by how each organization frames its purpose and values. This reinforces the need to consider DT initiatives not merely as technical processes but as a meaning-making exercise, deeply rooted in the unique normative logics that guide nonprofit work.

Technology Adoption, Implementation, and Strategic Framing

Although most organizations in the study had adopted digital tools to some extent, the rationale behind technology adoption varied significantly, reflecting different degrees of strategic framing, urgency, and integration. Some NPOs approached digital technologies reactively, often in response to external crises (such as COVID-19), while others engaged more proactively, embedding digital priorities into long-term planning and governance. NPO-E and NPO-J exemplify the reactive model of technology adoption, where DT initiatives were triggered mainly by the operational constraints of the pandemic. For these organizations, remote service delivery, online coordination, and digital record-keeping became needs rather than strategic initiatives. As the digital inclusion and project manager at NPO-J described: *"We had no choice. If we wanted to keep services running during lockdown, we had to figure out MS Teams, Zoom, for example, for managing shared folders; all of it, basically overnight."* Although these responses were rapid and resourceful, the technology itself was often layered on top of existing systems, without significant restructuring of internal processes. This led to some friction and limited long-term planning capacity. As such, DT here was primarily instrumental and problem-solving oriented, driven by situational need.

In contrast, NPO-C and NPO-F exemplified a proactive strategic framing of digital technology adoption. These organizations had already invested in digital infrastructure and governance mechanisms before the pandemic, viewing digital tools as a potential enabler to their operational model and social mission (in the digital era). For example, the financial manager at NPO-F explained: *"For us, tech is part of the plan. We are always looking for ways to do things smarter, reach further, and include more people. It is not just about fixing problems; it is about evolving."* This proactive attitude was often tied to broader organizational aspirations such as scalability, efficiency, and innovation. DT initiatives were thus integrated as strategic enablers, with investment in training, tools, and experimentation aligned with mission delivery.

However, between these poles of reactive and proactive adoption, several organizations demonstrated mixed or ambiguous framings. For instance, NPO-I adopted digital tools incrementally, often in response to specific operational bottlenecks, but without an articulated digital strategy. As their program manager described: *"Sometimes we just try things out. If it works, we keep it. If not, we move on. We do not have a digital roadmap or anything like that."* This pragmatic approach reflects situated learning and bottom-up experimentation and exposes potential risks in sustainability and alignment. For example, one key theme that emerged was a tension between technological experimentation and organizational stability. For NPOs already dealing with limited resources and volunteer turnover, the integration of new tools could disrupt routines, burden staff, or clash with ingrained practices. As the general manager of NPO-D noted: *"You cannot just throw tech at a charity and expect it to work. People have their ways of doing things, and change takes time."* This quote echoes the fragility of implementation in resource-constrained contexts, where even well-intentioned DT initiatives can pause without adequate support or alignment with work cultures. Taken together, these insights suggest that strategic framing plays a pivotal role in determining whether DT is experienced as a temporary adaptation, a burden, or a transformative opportunity. Where digital interest was aligned with mission goals and organizational planning, it often generated more sustained and meaningful change. Where it was reactive or fragmented, it risked being short-lived or poorly integrated.

Capacity-Building and Internal Capabilities

A central factor shaping how NPOs experience DT relates to their internal capacity and capability-building efforts. Across the cases, it appeared that the introduction of digital tools was often externally driven or operationally necessary, and the ability to make these tools "stick" depended largely on internal competencies, cultural attitudes, and learning mechanisms. This theme explores how organizations cultivated (or struggled to cultivate) the skills, mindsets, and structures needed to sustain DT initiatives (e.g., manage and govern them over time). Many NPOs in the study lacked formal IT departments or dedicated digital officers (which is not surprising). However, digital capability was often unevenly distributed, with a few individuals (usually senior staff or digitally-savvy volunteers) taking on disproportionate responsibility. For example, the general manager of NPO-D, a local history organization, emphasized the difficulty of training volunteers and adapting their workflows: "*We have brilliant volunteers, but many are retired and just not comfortable with tech. We try to show them how things work, but it is a slow process.*" In this case, internal resistance was not about ideology but about confidence, familiarity, and verve. This highlights the broader challenge of digital inequality within organizations, where not all staff or volunteers begin from the same level of digital readiness.

In contrast, some NPOs developed informal and low-pressure peer-learning mechanisms that proved effective in fostering capability. NPO-I, for instance, adopted a peer-led training approach, where more digitally literate volunteers offered workshops or one-on-one support to others. As their program manager explained: "*We did not want formal training sessions that feel corporate. Instead, we asked those who felt confident to just sit down with others and go through things together.*" This echoes an embedded and culturally sensitive approach to capacity-building, where digital learning is contextualized within the routines and relationships of an NPO. It also shows how horizontal learning structures can overcome formal resource limitations. From this perspective, some NPOs recognized early the need to embed digital upskilling into their operational model. The financial manager of NPO-F, for instance, said that the NPO incorporated basic tech training into volunteer onboarding: "*We realized that unless we supported people from day one, things would never move forward. It is not about pushing; it is about enabling.*" This proactive attitude reveals how capacity-building is not merely technical but also cultural and strategic. It requires an understanding of volunteer motivations, time constraints, and the specific digital demands of the NPO's work.

Another layer to internal capability involves knowledge flow and leadership style. In some NPOs, digital decision-making was centralized in one individual, which could accelerate progress but also create dependency. In others, particularly those with more distributed governance (e.g., NPO-G), tech knowledge was more diffused, creating broader engagement but sometimes slower application.

Notably, a few NPOs (NPO-B and NPO-E) expressed concerns about over-relying on external consultants or outsourcing partners. While outsourcing offered short-term solutions, it often failed to build internal confidence or self-sufficiency. As the coordinator of NPO-B remarked: "*They [the consultants] built us a system, but we did not know how to use it properly. When things broke down, we were stuck.*" This underscores a critical tension in DT initiatives. Although external expertise can catalyze adoption, long-term resilience often depends on internal capacity in NPOs. Therefore, decision-makers of NPOs should take this aspect into account and ensure sufficient knowledge is acquired accordingly. Overall, this theme suggests that the sustainability of DT in NPOs hinges on people more than (other organizations and not just) on tools. The step and depth of transformation are tied to how well NPOs cultivate internal skills, create space for learning, and embed digital practices into their everyday culture. It also points to the importance of slow, patient, and socially attuned approaches to change, especially in mission-driven organizations that rely on trust, shared values, and voluntary effort.

Stakeholder Pressures and the Role of Different Ecosystems

Beyond internal capabilities, the experience of DT within NPOs is profoundly shaped by their external environments. This includes formal partnerships, affiliations with national bodies, relationships with funders, and broader regulatory or policy contexts. These ecosystem dynamics can act as both enablers and constraints, depending on how they align with the goals, identity, and readiness of an NPO (and vice versa in some cases). Across the 10 cases, a recurring theme was the influence of umbrella organizations or networks, especially for those NPOs affiliated with national or sectoral bodies. For instance, NPO-B and NPO-E both mentioned their ties to larger, nationally recognized NPOs, which played a key role in guiding digital practices. For example, the leader of NPO-E noted: *"We get templates, guidance, and sometimes even access to shared digital tools from the national body. Although this is helpful for us, sometimes, we feel that it does not fully match our local reality."* This quote underscores the dual-edged nature of top-down support. Although national bodies could provide resources and legitimacy, local NPOs may struggle with the one-size-fits-all nature of these tools or guidelines. Similarly, funders were often cited as powerful shapers of digital direction. In several cases, it emerged that funding applications now require digital reporting, online service delivery, or proof of digital outreach. For example, NPO-G operates in the field of urban mobility and civic tech, and the Head of Partnerships reflected on this growing pressure: *"Funders want to see impact dashboards, metrics, online engagement. That is fair; however, this changes how we think about our work."* This aspect shows that some accountability demands from funders are digitizing the logic of service delivery, even in NPOs that were initially based on relational or offline models. These requirements can prompt strategic fulcrums, sometimes aligned with mission, sometimes more externally driven.

Other ecosystem pressures emerged from regulatory shifts and public sector policies, particularly around data protection (e.g., GDPR) or digital inclusion. The Founder of NPO-C, operating at the national level in financial literacy, shared: *"We had to rethink our digital outreach after the new privacy laws; it was not just a tech issue, it was about governance and trust."* This case exemplifies how DT in NPOs is not solely about introducing tools. Still, it includes rethinking processes, ethics, and accountability frameworks in response to external expectations (emerging as additional challenges that NPOs should handle anyway regardless of their status, at times preferable respect to for-profit contexts). In contrast, some NPOs struggled with a lack of ecosystemic support. For instance, NPO-H, focused on community arts, described feeling isolated from digital policy discourse: *"No one comes to us with offers or support. We are not part of the big discussions. We just try to make do."* Such experiences suggest that ecosystem support is unevenly distributed, appearing to privilege larger, more connected NPOs or those in high-profile sectors. This can deepen existing inequalities in the third sector, where smaller organizations risk being left behind in digital transitions. Besides, some organizations turned this challenge into an opportunity. For example, NPO-J leveraged regional partnerships to build a digital inclusion program: *"We worked with the council, a tech company, and a university. Alone, we could not do much, but together we managed to train over 60 older adults in digital skills."* This example shows a collaborative model toward DT initiatives, where ecosystem actors co-create solutions that align with local needs and capacities. Hence, the role of the ecosystem is pivotal in shaping DT trajectories in NPOs. External actors can offer critical support, resources, and legitimacy, but also introduce pressures, constraints, or mismatches within realities. The ability of an NPO to navigate, negotiate, and selectively align with its ecosystem appears crucial to building resilient and context-sensitive digital strategies.

Tensions, Trade-Off, and Adaptive Strategies

So far, besides well-known themes about DT and factors characterizing NPOs, evidence shows that the DT process in NPOs is not a linear or uniformly positive journey. Across the 10 case studies, several tensions, compromises, and strategic adaptations emerged as NPOs tried to balance technological change with their core missions, operational realities, and stakeholder expectations. This further theme captures the challenges that arise when NPOs must make opposite choices; for example, between speed and inclusion, or between innovation and continuity, as they navigate their transformation pathways. From this perspective, one recurring tension emerged concerning time and capacity constraints. Many NPOs operate with stretched staff and heavy dependence on volunteers, making the adoption of new systems or platforms an additional burden. For example, the project manager of NPO-J explained: *"We did not want to go too fast, we could lose people on the way. Not everyone here is confident with tech, and we needed to swiftness it up to avoid alienating them."* This quote echoes a widespread concern for NPOs, that is, there is a possibility that moving too quickly with digital tools may risk excluding individuals who are less confident or experienced, particularly volunteers or service users with limited digital literacy.

A second pattern concerns the strategic ambiguity around technology investments. Several NPOs appeared feeling pressure to adopt digital tools, especially in response to the expectations of their founders or peer practices, but without clear frameworks to evaluate long-term implications. NPO-D, for example, adopted a new system to track service users, but later realized it had limited internal expertise to maintain or customize it. The General Manager of such an NPO noticed: *"It sounded great on paper, but now we are stuck with a tool that is too complex for what we really need.*" This aligns with the broader tension between innovation and operational alignment, where DT initiatives that appear beneficial at a strategic level may prove misaligned with day-to-day NPO practices. Trade-offs were also evident in how such initiatives reshaped service delivery models. For example, NPO-E transitioned part of its social support activities to online consultations during the pandemic. Overall, this transition benefited from an increased reach, concurrently creating new barriers. The Leader explained: "*We found that some of our older beneficiaries simply would not engage through Zoom.*" This evidence, as seen in the case of NPO-A, which committed to integrating digital community screenings, highlights the friction between efficiency gains and inclusion mandates. From this perspective, DT initiatives may also deepen existing exclusions if not managed carefully. Additionally, NPOs had to weigh internal resistance and change management costs. NPO-F, for instance, encountered significant reluctance among long-standing staff when introducing a cloud-based filing system. "*We did not realize how emotional this would be. People felt their way of working was being erased.*" Although this resistance was eventually overcome through informal peer mentoring, the case illustrates that emotional and cultural dimensions of change cannot be underestimated, particularly in NPOs with strong legacy values and practices.

Interestingly, to manage these tensions, most NPOs developed adaptive strategies that blended pragmatism and creativity. NPO-I, for example, used phased roll-outs for new tools and deliberately paired digital-savvy volunteers with less experienced staff in a user-friendly system. Others, like NPO-C, adopted a "test-and-learn" approach, piloting tech solutions in limited "departments" of the NPOs before wider implementation. Outsourcing also emerged as a typical adaptive response. Several NPOs (e.g., NPO-B and NPO-F) relied on external IT consultants or web developers on a need basis, bypassing the need for full-time digital staff. However, these adaptations often emerged reactively rather than through formalized digital strategies. Specifically, it seems that no NPOs had robust risk assessments or sustainability plans for their digital tools. Even in cases where DT initiatives were pursued proactively (e.g., NPO-C, NPO-G), the organizations acknowledged limits in their ability to predict downstream effects. The founder of NPO-C remarked: "*We have digitized a lot (we consider ourselves a born digital NPO), but honestly, we are still catching up with what that means for governance and data responsibility.*" What emerges, then, is a representation of DT as a negotiated process, shaped by a continuous balancing act between constraints and aspirations. At times, NPOs are not passive adopters of digital technology; they selectively adopt, resist, adapt, and repurpose tools in line with their missions, values, and operational logics. Conversely, this process brings new costs, generating friction, trade-offs, and often unintended consequences. These insights underscore the importance of viewing DT in NPOs as a complex social and organizational shift, besides technical upgrades, requiring NPOs to redesign new forms of reflection, leadership, and organizational learning.

5.4 Final Considerations

To consolidate the empirical insights generated through the cross-case analysis, the emerging coding structure is summarized in Table 5.2. This table provides a structured overview of the inductive logic underpinning the identification of core themes across the 10 case studies. Moving from first-order concepts to second-order themes and then to aggregate dimensions, it offers an interpretive bridge between field data and conceptual abstraction (Corbin & Strauss, 1990; Gioia et al., 2013). This evidence could serve as a structuring lens to interpret the diverse conditions under which NPOs engage in DT initiatives. Notably, four aggregate dimensions emerged from this process, representing empirically grounded preconditions that enable, constrain, or shape DT trajectories in NPOs. These aggregate dimensions, *Operational Settings*, *Willingness and Readiness*, *Ecosystemic Settings*, and

Table 5.2 Coding structure summary

First-order concepts	Second-order themes	Aggregate dimensions
Limited funding opportunities	Financial and Operational Resources	Operational Settings
Cost of facilities and services		
Dependence on external grants		
Constraints in service locations	Spatial and Structural Adaptability	
Need to adapt spaces to social mission		
Variation in area served (local to national)	Scope and Mission Consistency	
Alignment with social mission		
Shift to cashless and online transactions	Digitalization of Service Operations	Willingness and Readiness
Digitalization of frontline services		
Adoption of cloud-based tools	Technology Infrastructure	
Use of integrated digital suites		
Limited data analytics capacity	Information and Data Management	
Fragmented information systems		
Support from public institutions (councils, universities)	Institutional and Peer Support	Ecosystemic Settings
Partnerships with peer NPOs or private actors		
Pressure from inflation, policy, and external funding logic	External Contextual Pressures	
Diverse target populations and user profiles	Demographic Complexity	
Overlapping roles and multitasking	Internal Collaboration Dynamics	Human-Cultural Factors
Informal internal coordination		
Stress, burnout, and volunteer fatigue	Workload and Emotional Pressures	
Need for better task distribution		
Engagement of skilled volunteers	Volunteer and Human Capital Management	
Retention challenges		

Human-Cultural Factors (see Table 5.2), highlight the interplay between organizational configurations, technological capabilities, contextual dependencies, and internal social dynamics. Accordingly, as thematic areas, they can serve as practical guidance for decision-makers and organizational leaders in NPOs approaching DT. They outline key domains that must be considered when designing, implementing, or scaling DT initiatives, offering insight into how to anticipate challenges, allocate resources more effectively, and foster institutional alignment.

Examining Table 5.2, although these dimensions appear analytically distinct, they often intersect in practice, generating complex configurations of readiness and resistance (frequently reinforcing or constraining one another in dynamic ways). Specifically, *Operational Settings* refers to the material and structural characteristics of an NPO, including financial stability, access to adequate facilities, and the alignment between operational reach and mission coherence. These conditions determine the ability of an NPO to invest in and sustain DT initiatives while mediating tensions between innovation, continuity, and survival. Recognizing these aspects in advance can help managers assess feasibility and avoid overextension in DT agendas.

Willingness and Readiness refers to the attitude of an NPO toward digital innovation, given both the mindset toward digital innovation and its actual technological position. This includes the use of digital tools in everyday operations, infrastructure quality (e.g., cloud platforms), and data management capabilities. Practically, readiness extends technology availability, involving also the evaluation of cultural and operational preparedness to embed digital practices into workflows and service delivery. For practitioners, this means assessing digital maturity beyond tool adoption.

Ecosystemic Settings refers to the institutional, networked, and macro-environmental forces surrounding an NPO. These include partnerships with public and private actors, regulatory and funding environments, and demographic pressures related to beneficiaries. Although these factors often lie beyond the direct control of an NPO, they significantly influence the timing, scope, and viability of DT initiatives. Engaging strategically with these contextual elements, through advocacy, cooperation, and adaptive planning, can enhance resilience and innovation capacity.

Human-Cultural Factors refers to the interpersonal, emotional, and behavioral aspects that govern how individuals experience and enact change. These include collaboration patterns, informal governance structures, volunteer engagement, and stress or overload management. As DT often disrupts routines and roles, these elements can become friction points or enabling forces. Managers must then consider such human and cultural bases beyond the technological and structural side of DT.

In short, these findings can support NPOs with guidance to navigate their digital journeys in context-sensitive ways. Then, Chap. 6 ultimately integrates this empirical evidence to propose a series of interpretive insights and research directions.

References

Cipriano, M., Za, S., & Bednar, P. M. (2023). The digital transformation of non-profit organisations in the United Kingdom: A multiple case study United Kingdom. In *ITAIS 2023 Proceedings*. AIS Electronic Library. https://aisel.aisnet.org/itais2023/10

Corbin, J. M., & Strauss, A. (1990). Grounded theory research: Procedures, canons, and evaluative criteria. *Qualitative Sociology, 13*(1), 3–21. https://doi.org/10.1007/BF00988593

Eisenhardt, K. M. (1989). Building theories from case study research. *The Academy of Management Review, 14*(4), 532. https://doi.org/10.2307/258557

Gioia, D. A., Corley, K. G., & Hamilton, A. L. (2013). Seeking qualitative rigor in inductive research. *Organizational Research Methods, 16*(1), 15–31. https://doi.org/10.1177/1094428112452151

Yin, R. K. (2018). *Case study research and applications: Design and methods. Climate Change 2013 – The Physical Science Basis* (6th ed.). Cambridge University Press. https://www.cambridge.org/core/product/identifier/CBO9781107415324A009/type/book_part

Chapter 6
Discussion

6.1 Overview

This chapter integrates the findings presented across the preceding chapters to offer a cohesive understanding of how NPOs engage with DT processes. By revisiting the conceptual, taxonomical, strategic, and empirical contributions of the study, it echoes the complexity and heterogeneity of DT processes in the nonprofit domain. Accordingly, the chapter aims to articulate the patterns, preconditions, and tensions that shape how NPOs navigate digital innovation amid resource constraints, mission-driven mandates, and evolving institutional environments. Structured as a synthesis that bridges conceptual abstraction and practice-oriented insights, the chapter ends by proposing a research agenda grounded in the findings. It outlines directions for future inquiry into the evolving relationship between digital technologies, organizational change, and social value creation in NPOs.

6.2 Summarizing Core Contributions

The core ambition of this book has been to investigate how DT initiatives unfold within NPOs, with particular attention to their organizational, strategic, and ecosystemic dimensions. Adopting a multilevel and empirically grounded approach, the study conceptualizes DT not as a linear or purely technological process, but rather as a context-sensitive reconfiguration of structures, practices, and relationships. The analyses draw on perspectives from strategic management and information systems, guided by the following overarching research question: *How do NPOs initiate, interpret, and enact DT processes across strategic, organizational, and ecosystemic dimensions?*

M. Cipriano, *Digital Transformation in Non-profit Organizations*, SpringerBriefs in Information Systems,
https://doi.org/10.1007/978-3-032-20937-5_6

To answer this question, the book has been structured into five analytical chapters, each contributing a distinct layer of insight. *Chapter 2* established the conceptual and theoretical foundations of the study. It critically reviewed the literature discussing DT in NPOs strictly, highlighting analytical fragmentation, conceptual ambiguities, and limited cross-disciplinary fertilization. The chapter proposed a system-level perspective that integrates organizational change, digital service logic, and information systems research.

Chapter 3 introduced a taxonomy based on a classification of 124 peer-reviewed articles and articulated a theoretical framework comprising 5 dimensions and 29 distinct values describing DT initiatives in NPOs. Then, a cluster analysis was conducted to uncover emergent organizational profiles, revealing nine different patterns of DT engagement. From these clusters and related overarching archetypes, three overarching profiles (of NPOs toward DT) are provisionally identified as *Explorers*, *Pragmatists*, and *Traditionalists*, each reflecting different levels of strategic intent, innovation posture, and mission alignment. This classification offers a comparative lens for understanding the heterogeneity of DT trajectories across NPOs.

Chapter 4 advanced a strategic framework based on propositions derived from the previous chapters. Such a conceptualization also led to argument three core logics of engagement with DT in NPOs: *Alignment*, *Integration*, and *Configuration*, which represent distinct ways in which organizations navigate the tensions between digital opportunities, mission fulfillment, and operational constraints.

Chapter 5 presented the empirical findings of semistructured interviews from 10 UK-based case studies, analyzed through a grounded coding approach. The analysis revealed four aggregate dimensions: *Operational Settings*, *Willingness and Readiness*, *Ecosystemic Settings*, and *Human-Cultural Factors*. These were inferred as empirically grounded preconditions that shape how DT processes unfold in practice.

By and large, these contributions provide a granular and context-sensitive account of DT phenomena in NPOs. The book moves beyond deterministic or capability-based accounts by conceptualizing DT as a negotiated, dynamic, and multi-actor process. Thus, it contributes to broader debates on hybrid organizing, digitally enabled change, and innovation under constraint in mission-driven settings.

6.3 Integrative Synthesis and Emerging Tensions

By integrating the multilayered findings and empirically grounded understanding presented across this book, a series of key synthesis points and tensions emerge. In particular, key tensions that contribute to explaining how NPOs engage with DT processes concern their positioning through *(1) Aspirations* vs. *Capacities; (2) Strategic Intent* vs. *Operational Realities; (3) Mission Alignment* vs. *Technology Adoption; and (4) External Pressure* vs. *Internal Control.*

First, a central tension is between aspiration and the actual capacity of NPOs. Many NPOs seem to express intent to innovate but are still constrained by limited operational and human resources. This gap was already highlighted in the contrast between "NPOs' profiles toward DT" (e.g., Explorers, Pragmatists, Traditionalists) and their actual levels of readiness.

Second, further tension is evident in the divergence between strategic logics (e.g., Integration or Configuration) and foundational readiness levels (e.g., infrastructure gaps or staff overload), where NPOs may fail if key preconditions (such as infrastructure, skills, or cultural support) are absent or underdeveloped.

Third, NPOs are often driven by deeply held social purposes. Nevertheless, attempts to implement a DT initiative sometimes create friction when they are perceived to divert from mission-oriented practices or core values.

Fourth, ecosystemic pressures, such as shifts in funding models or policy environments, directly affect the internal decision-making of NPOs in unpredictable ways. Shifting policy frameworks, funding mechanisms, and technological trends impose ecosystemic volatility that lies beyond managerial control. This unpredictability often collides with internal decision-making timelines and capacity.

The NPOs' profiles derived from Chap. 3 (Explorers, Pragmatists, Traditionalists) could serve to mediate these tensions. In particular, it emerged that (NPOs acting as) Explorers tend to adopt more integrative or configurational logics, leveraging strong (favorable) preconditions. Traditionalists, by contrast, often operate within narrower strategic scopes, constrained by weaker readiness levels and more rigid operational settings. Pragmatists exemplify a middle path, selectively investing in DT while preserving organizational continuity.

This synthesis highlights that DT is less about technology adoption per se, and more about how NPOs manage alignment across strategy, structure, mission, and external environment. It underscores the negotiated and iterative nature of DT, shaped by ongoing recalibrations between ambition, values, and resource realities.

6.4 Navigating DT in NPOs: A Multilayered Framework

To consolidate and visualize the synthesis of this study, this section presents a multilevel conceptual framework (see Fig. 6.1) that integrates the empirical and theoretical insights developed throughout the book. The framework adopts a center → shell architecture, representing how DT in NPOs emerges from core enabling conditions, is shaped by strategic choices, embodied in organizational profiles, and interpreted through overarching theoretical lenses.

First Layer (Core): Preconditions for DT At the heart of the framework are the four empirically grounded preconditions for DT identified in Chap. 5. These conditions form the practical starting point for any transformation effort and either enable or constrain change related to DT initiatives. That is, *Operational Settings* (including financial resources, physical infrastructure, and mission-scope alignment); *Willingness and Readiness* (covering digital mindsets, technological practices, and internal digital capabilities); *Ecosystemic Settings* (such as institutional partnerships,

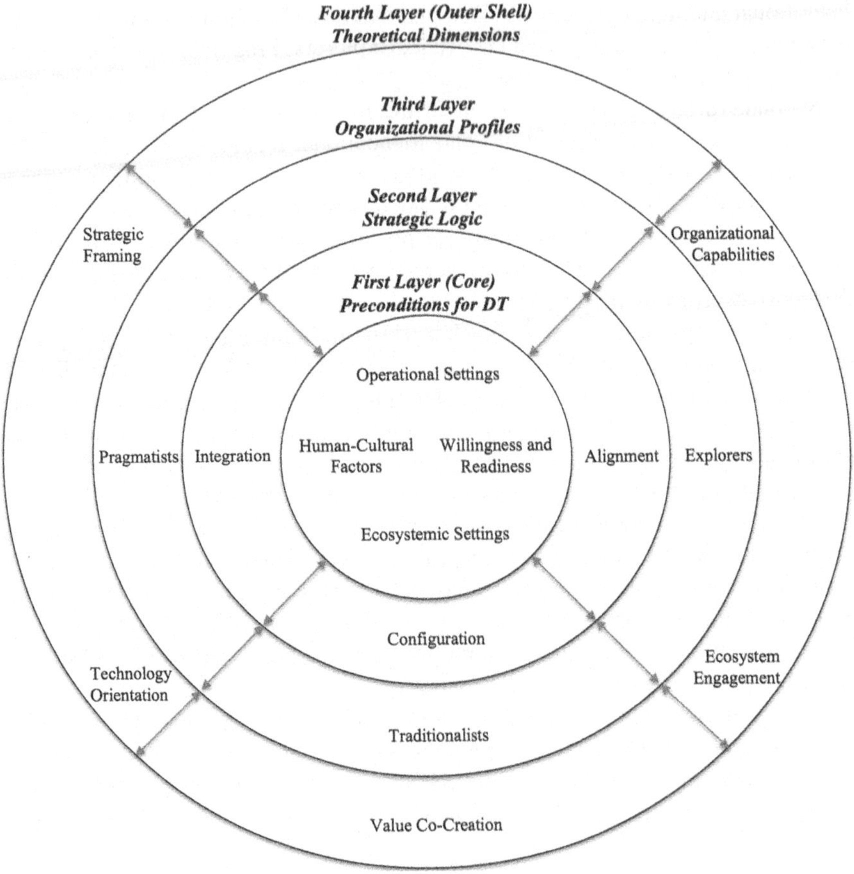

Fig. 6.1 A multilayered conceptual framework for examining DT in NPOs

funding dynamics, and external pressures); and *Human-Cultural Factors* (including staff engagement, collaboration practices, and emotional resilience).

Second Layer: Strategic Logics Surrounding the core preconditions are the three strategic logics derived from Chap. 4, representing alternative pathways through which NPOs respond to their starting conditions toward DT. The different strategic pathways are labeled as *Alignment* (representing NPOs using digital tools to reinforce and support the existing mission and practices); *Integration* (representing NPOs that systematically embed digital capabilities across services and administrative processes); and *Configuration* (representing NPOs that reconfigure structures, routines, and relationships to enable new digital service models). These logics are not fixed categories but adaptive strategies that can evolve in response to changes in preconditions.

Third Layer: Organizational Profiles Enveloping the strategic logics are the organizational profiles inferred from Chap. 3, which capture the diverse ways NPOs operationalize DT. That is, *Explorers* (representing NPOs acting as proactive adopters with innovation-focused strategies), *Pragmatists* (representing NPOs acting as selective implementers balancing innovation with established practices), and *Traditionalists* (representing NPOs acting as cautious or constrained actors with limited digital ambition). From this perspective, profiles mediate the relationship between strategic intent and readiness conditions, influencing how logics are enacted in practice.

Fourth Layer (Outer Shell): Theoretical Dimensions Encircling the entire model are the five conceptual dimensions mainly inferred from synthesizing the literature in Chap. 3, and reframed according to the overall comprehension developed throughout the book, functioning as boundary conditions and interpretive lenses for understanding DT in NPOs: *Strategic Framing*, *Organizational Capabilities*, *Technology Orientation*, *Ecosystem Engagement*, and *Value Co-creation*. These dimensions contextualize the empirical findings within broader academic discourse, ensuring that the framework can inform both scholarly debates and practical decision-making.

Figure 6.1 depicts this architecture as a series of concentric layers. At the innermost core lie the preconditions, which represent the foundational conditions enabling or constraining DT in NPOs. These are encircled by the strategic logics, illustrating how NPOs act upon their starting conditions to shape DT pathways. Surrounding the strategic logics are the NPOs' profiles, which mediate the relationship between strategic intent and readiness, influencing how digital change is enacted in practice. Enveloping the entire structure is the outer shell of theoretical dimensions, which serves as a conceptual boundary and interpretive frame, linking empirical realities to broader academic discourse. Moreover, bidirectional arrows connect each layer, emphasizing that DT in NPOs is an iterative, nonlinear process in which outer layers influence (and are, in turn, influenced by) the core. This integrative configuration captures the dynamic, context-sensitive, and multilayered nature of DT in the nonprofit domain.

6.5 Implications and Concluding Reflections

This work aimed to examine the organizational, strategic, and ecosystemic conditions that shape how NPOs engage with DT phenomena. The findings suggest that DT initiatives in the nonprofit domain go far beyond processes originally contemplated through the adoption of new technologies or digitizing existing services (which, for NPOs, generally already represents a significant investment). Instead, it emerges through a complex interplay of mission coherence, resource constraints, human dynamics, and environmental pressures. This nuanced understanding gives rise to a set of theoretical and managerial implications that, while already embedded throughout the preceding discussion, can be briefly summarized here.

From a theoretical perspective, the study contributes to IS and organizational literature by advancing a multilevel conceptualization of DT in NPOs. Rather than treating NPOs as lagging or passive adopters, the layered framework (see Fig. 6.1) recognizes them as active agents navigating transformation through hybrid logics. It integrates preconditions, strategic responses, organizational profiles, and conceptual boundaries, offering a richer and more context-sensitive foundation to interpret DT phenomena in mission-driven settings. It also invites future research to adopt interpretive, ecosystemic, and sociotechnical perspectives, rather than assuming linear or capability-based models of change.

From a managerial standpoint, the findings offer actionable insights for NPO leaders and decision-makers. First, they suggest that a successful digital strategy cannot be copied from for-profit models but must emerge from the organization's mission, internal dynamics, and readiness conditions. Second, DT initiatives should be approached as adaptive and participatory processes rather than top-down technological deployments. Attention to emotional climate, workload distribution, and informal coordination practices is key to sustaining momentum and engagement. Third, ecosystem engagement is not a peripheral activity but central to DT, requiring NPOs to cultivate partnerships, navigate institutional logics, and seek alignment between external support and internal capacity.

Ultimately, this study invites a shift in perspective from seeing DT as a linear solution to operational inefficiencies to recognizing it as a dynamic process of organizational learning and negotiation. It is through such a lens that both scholars and practitioners may better understand and support the digital futures of NPOs.

6.6 Future Directions for Studying DT in NPOs

This work has unpacked the dynamics of DT in NPOs through a combination of analyses and strategic reasoning. The resulting integrated framework (see Fig. 6.1) represents DT in NPOs as a context-sensitive, tension-filled, and strategically navigated phenomenon. Drawing on these findings, this section outlines a research agenda that can guide future investigations into the evolving interplay between digital innovation and organizational transformation in NPOs. The agenda is structured around four interrelated directions. First, *Investigating DT Readiness as a Situated Construct*. While readiness is often treated as a checklist of capabilities, the findings of this work reveal that readiness in NPOs is deeply situated in organizational mission, culture, and constraints (e.g., findings showed that DT efforts began not with a formal strategy but (oftentimes) with everyday improvisations by staff or volunteers). Thus, DT readiness for NPOs should be reconceptualized as a situated and evolving process shaped by material, cultural, and experiential factors (Orlikowski, 2000; Weick, 1995), where future research should explore:

1. How does readiness evolve through trial-and-error or experiential learning in NPOs (Weick, 1995)?
2. How do perceptions of readiness evolve over time through learning-by-doing?
3. What informal infrastructures (e.g., people, habits, routines) underpin DT efforts in NPOs?

Such inquiries can advance more relational and processual theories of readiness in hybrid or constrained nonprofit contexts. Second, *Exploring Strategic Logics as Dynamic Patterns.* This study conceptualized Alignment, Integration, and Configuration as distinct logics of DT engagement by NPOs (that should be explored as dynamic and context-contingent patterns, not static categories). Future work can build on this by examining:

1. Under what conditions (e.g., organizational triggers or ecosystem events) do NPOs shift from one logic to another (Bharadwaj et al., 2013)? And which one leads to strategy shifts?
2. How do strategic logics relate to the success/failure of DT initiatives?
3. What role do leaders, funders, or users play in activating different DT logics?

Such research could unpack the strategic reorientation processes in mission-driven organizations facing digital disruption. Then a third tension concerns *Analyzing Ecosystemic Pressures and Collaboration Mechanisms.* External actors (e.g., public agencies, peer NPOs, funders, tech firms) were shown to shape DT in NPOs significantly. Understanding how external institutions, funding logics, and collaborative networks shape DT practices remains a priority (Adner, 2017). Thus, future studies may explore:

1. How do ecosystemic pressures vary across national or regional contexts?
2. What forms of "digital" inter-organizational collaboration (which digital ecosystems) are emerging in the third sector? And how do NPOs maintain agency while engaging in asymmetric "digital" partnerships?
3. How do power asymmetries and legitimacy dynamics influence interactions among the actors belonging to the ecosystem of an NPO (Adner, 2017)?

This direction can contribute to expanding the understanding of multiactor and cross-sectoral digital ecosystems in nonprofit work. Moreover, a fourth direction refers to *Rethinking Human and Cultural Dynamics of Digital Change.* The empirical data revealed the often invisible, emotional, and behavioral dimensions of DT in NPOs (which shape how people respond to change). Future research should consider:

1. How do "digital" changes (triggering stress, burnout, or overload) reshape the identity of NPO workers and volunteers (Sarker et al., 2013; Tarafdar et al., 2013)? And which mechanisms shape digital adaptation in NPOs?
2. What are the long-term effects of unaddressed emotional stressors? And which practices promote psychological safety and digital resilience in NPOs (Edmondson & Lei, 2014)?
3. How do values and identity interrelate with digital innovation in NPOs?

This further direction can contribute to shedding light on sensitive human-centered and ethical approaches to DT research in NPOs and beyond. Overall, these directions aim to suggest that future research should continue moving beyond technology-centric and capability-driven models. Particularly concerning NPOs, there is a need for interpretive, contextual, and cross-disciplinary approaches that center the unique constraints and opportunities of the nonprofit sector. By doing so, scholars can better theorize how technology mediates mission-driven work.

In addition to the outlined directions, future research should also engage in longitudinal and comparative studies that explore how DT trajectories unfold over time across different institutional, geographic, or organizational contexts. There is also a need to understand better how nondigital factors, such as trust, ethics, and community embeddedness, interrelate with technological change in shaping outcomes. Finally, studies that adopt participatory, design-oriented, or ethnographic methodologies could enrich our understanding of DT as a lived experience, offering insights that are both academically robust and practically relevant to NPOs on the ground.

6.7 Closing Remarks

This final chapter has sought to unify the theoretical, taxonomical, strategic, and empirical strands developed throughout the book into a coherent understanding of DT in NPOs. The proposed integrative framework and research agenda mark an effort to move beyond fragmented or overly deterministic interpretations of DT, offering a model that is both analytically rigorous and sensitive to the distinct realities of nonprofit work. Examining DT initiatives in NPOs is a social, strategic, and institutional project beyond exploring the technical system characterizing DT processes. As such, it requests interdisciplinary inquiry, organizational reflexivity, and a critical awareness of context. Although this book offers one contribution to that effort, it is hoped that the reflections, frameworks, and agenda proposed here will serve as a springboard for further dialogue and discovery at the intersection of digital innovation and mission-driven organizing.

References

Adner, R. (2017). Ecosystem as structure: An actionable construct for strategy. *Journal of Management, 43*(1), 39–58. https://doi.org/10.1177/0149206316678451

Bharadwaj, A., El Sawy, O. A., Pavlou, P. A., & Venkatraman, N. (2013). Digital business strategy: Toward a next generation of insights. *MIS Quarterly, 37*(2), 471–482. https://doi.org/10.25300/MISQ/2013/37:2.3

Edmondson, A. C., & Lei, Z. (2014). Psychological safety: The history, renaissance, and future of an interpersonal construct. *Annual Review of Organizational Psychology and Organizational Behavior, 1*(1), 23–43. https://doi.org/10.1146/annurev-orgpsych-031413-091305

Orlikowski, W. J. (2000). Using technology and constituting structures: A practice lens for studying technology in organizations. *Organization Science, 11*(4), 404–428. https://doi.org/10.1287/orsc.11.4.404.14600

Sarker, S., Chatterjee, S., & Xiao, X. (2013). How "sociotechnical" is our IS research? An assessment and possible ways forward. In *Proceedings of the 34th international conference on information systems (ICIS), Milan, Italy*. Accessed 7 August 2025.

Tarafdar, M., Gupta, A., & Turel, O. (2013). The dark side of information technology use. *Information Systems Journal, 23*(3), 269–275. https://doi.org/10.1111/isj.12015

Weick, K. E. (1995). *Sensemaking in organizations* (Vol. 3, No. 10.1002). Sage Publications. Accessed 7 August 2025.

Chapter 7
Conclusions

Digital transformation (DT) is no longer confined to the realm of technological innovation; it now permeates organizational strategy, structure, and practice across all sectors. While the private and public sectors have received sustained scholarly attention, the transformation pathways of nonprofit organizations (NPOs) have remained comparatively underexplored. This book has sought to redress that imbalance by systematically examining the dynamics, challenges, and opportunities of DT in the nonprofit domain.

Through a combination of bibliometric analysis, thematic synthesis, comparative framework evaluation, and qualitative case research, the work has built a comprehensive and multilevel understanding of how mission-driven organizations experience and enact digital change. Central to this effort is the multilayered conceptual framework, which places foundational preconditions at the center, links them to strategic logics of engagement, and situates organizational profiles within a bounded set of theoretical dimensions. This architecture provides both analytical clarity for researchers and a practical roadmap for decision-makers navigating the complexities of DT in NPOs.

Several distinctive contributions emerge. First, the book differentiates NPO-specific DT pathways from dominant for-profit models, emphasizing the role of governance structures, mission orientation, and resource constraints in shaping strategic choices. Second, it introduces an integrative conceptual framework that accounts for the interplay between organizational readiness, strategic intent, and environmental conditions. Third, it outlines some key tensions, such as the balance between mission fulfillment and digital innovation, that underpin decision-making in NPO contexts.

The implications are manifold. For managers and practitioners, the findings offer actionable insights into aligning DT strategies with organizational mission, strengthening adaptive capacity, and fostering ecosystems favorable to sustainable innovation. For policymakers and funders, they highlight the importance of enabling

M. Cipriano, *Digital Transformation in Non-profit Organizations*, SpringerBriefs in Information Systems,
https://doi.org/10.1007/978-3-032-20937-5_7

environments that recognize the distinct needs of the nonprofit sector. For researchers, the book arranges a clear agenda for future inquiry, including comparative studies across sectors, longitudinal assessments of DT paths, and deeper investigation into the cultural dimensions of DT change.

By placing NPOs at the center of the DT conversation, this work underscores their critical role in addressing societal challenges in a digitally mediated world. The hope is that it will serve as a catalyst for both scholarly engagement and practical innovation, contributing to a richer, more inclusive understanding of how organizations dedicated to public and community good can sustain and enhance their missions in an era of continual digital evolution.

The manufacturer's authorised representative in the EU is Springer Nature Customer Service Centre GmbH, Europaplatz 3, 69115 Heidelberg, Germany. If you have any concerns regarding our products, please contact ProductSafety@springernature.com

Printed and bound by CPI Group (UK) Ltd, Croydon, CR0 4YY
05/10/2026
02228047-0002